NORWICH
IN 100 DATES

KINDRA JONES

The History Press

To my parents,
who imparted to me a love of learning
and taught me to listen to the lessons of the past.

First published 2016

The History Press
The Mill, Brimscombe Port
Stroud, Gloucestershire, GL5 2QG
www.thehistorypress.co.uk

© Kindra Jones 2016

The right of Kindra Jones to be identified as the Author
of this work has been asserted in accordance with the
Copyright, Designs and Patents Act 1988.

British Library Cataloguing in Publication Data.
A catalogue record for this book is available from the British Library.

ISBN 978 0 7509 6143 1

Typesetting and origination by The History Press

Printed and bound by TJ International, Padstow, Cornwall

Contents

Acknowledgements

I am indebted to my partner, Martin, for his support and patience, especially during moments of exasperation when a particular date I was after eluded me.

I consider myself very lucky to count amongst my friends some very fine historians, to whom I am grateful for helping to show a London girl the beauty of Norwich and the county of Norfolk. Some readers may already know of Neil Storey, a first-class academic with an ability to bring the past to life in a uniquely inspiring fashion. And Dave Tonge, the Yarnsmith of Norwich, whose skill at weaving a tale captures both the young and old alike, holding them in awe and surreptitiously imparting nuggets of historical fact wrapped in ancient knowledge.

With special thanks to Adam Jones and Jason Mayfield-Lewis for their help and support.

In seeking out specific dates I would like to extend my thanks to the staff at the Norfolk Record Office, Norfolk Museum Service and Norwich HEART for their detailed research and assistance with my enquiries.

My gratitude also goes to Matilda Richards for taking a risk and giving me this opportunity, and all at The History Press for their help and support.

Introduction

'What a grand, higgledy-piggledy, sensible old place Norwich is!'

J.B. Priestley

Norwich has a fascinating history filled with remarkable events and people. During its past Norwich has produced best-selling writers, stood up against kings and for human rights. As a pioneering city it saw the first provincial newspaper published, was the first local authority to install a computer, had the first female Lord Mayor, and continues with its writing tradition as the first English City of Literature. Of course, there have been darker moments in Norwich's past too. Its people have survived plagues, raids, fire and floods. The power struggle between the city and Church saw people die, property damaged and even resulted in the Pope excommunicating the city.

But when did it all begin?

The very first evidence of people in Norwich dates back to Palaeolithic finds at Carrow Road, and the earliest structures found indicate a settlement of some type in the late Neolithic/early Bronze Age. Although people may have occupied the site of Norwich, it was only after the Romans that the area really began to thrive.

Just south of modern Norwich can be found Caistor St Edmunds. First an Iceni stronghold, it became the Roman capital of East Anglia following the defeat of Boudicca's tribe. The Roman ruins are remarkably intact since the area diminished in importance following the Roman occupation. It seems the Romans weren't so interested in the area where the city is based now, but if the popular rhyme is true, then Caistor's demise led to the development of Norwich: 'Caistor was a city when Norwich was none, Norwich was built from Caistor stone.'

It was during the Anglo-Saxon period that Norwich came into its own. The existence of pottery from the continent points to long-distance trade right near the beginning. However, being close to the sea came with its own dangers and the area was subject to Viking raids. To begin with, the King of East Anglia, Edmund, led the resistance, but his death marked the beginning of Dane rule in a large part of England. After some struggle the rule returned to the Saxons, and those remaining in the city settled alongside the native inhabitants. Their presence can still be seen in Norwich today in Danish street names. Coins from the time of King Æthelstan have been found marked '*Norvic*', indicating the presence of a mint and showing Norwich's growing importance.

The arrival of the Normans not only saw the building of the castle and cathedral, but also the city wall. With twelve main gates and forty towers, the city walls enclosed an area larger than any other town in England, or even the City of London. Originally built for taxation and defensive purposes, they were also a testament to the proudly defended self-governance of Norwich and a foreboding greeting to any visitor. The medieval period saw huge economic growth in the area and this was demonstrated most obviously in the building of churches. At one point Norwich could boast one church for every week of the year (and perhaps rather more tellingly one pub for every day!). Norwich continued to flourish, mainly on the success of the textile trade and with help from the Strangers, immigrants to the area from the Low Countries.

'Either a city in an orchard or an orchard in a city, so equally are houses and trees blended in it.'

Thomas Fuller, *Worthies of England*, 1662

Although Norwich for much of its history was the second city of England, it was also known as a city of gardens. Following the fashions of London, Norwich developed a series of pleasure gardens, most likely the earliest being My Lord's Garden in the 1660s. A modest entrance fee would give the visitor an escape from city life and access to a variety of entertainments from music and exotic animals to the latest popular novelty. At the end of the eighteenth century these were the flights of the 'aerostatic globe' (hot-air balloons) and Norwich had a spate of them, with tickets priced to suit a range of pockets. In 1785 Major John Money, in an attempt to raise funds for the Norfolk and Norwich Hospital, took off from Ranelagh Gardens but a rogue wind took him out to sea and it was many hours before he was at last rescued.

It is often joked that Norwich missed the Industrial Revolution, and although it is true that textile production flourished elsewhere as Norwich's waned, other industries and companies emerged over the nineteenth and twentieth centuries to become household names: Colman's Mustard, Bernard Matthew's 'bootiful' turkeys and Norwich Union are a few examples.

Norwich continues to be a celebration of individuality, creativity and eccentricity. What follows is just a sample of these from sporting victories to the peculiarities of mundane life to the local impact of national and international events.

Kindra Jones,
2016

NORWICH
IN 100 DATES

14 October

On this day Gyrth Godwinson, Earl of East Anglia and younger brother of King Harold II, fought and died at the Battle of Hastings. His death is recorded on the Bayeux Tapestry.

Originally Norwic (or Northwic) referred to just one area of several based on the banks of the river Wensum, but as the areas grew and merged the name dominated, referring to the borough as a whole. In 1004 Sweyn Forkbeard, the King of Denmark, sacked Norwich and when the town re-emerged the area south of the river became the new centre. The earl's palace was based in the centre of the borough at Tombland (meaning open space in Old English), where the crossroads made it an easy focal point for the Saxon town. It was here that the principal market thrived, and by the time of the conquest there were about thirty churches in the city.

The Normans were quick to assert their power and the market was moved to be closer to the new power centre of the city: the castle. A few years later, the palace was demolished to make way for the cathedral.

1 August

When King William the Conqueror met on this day with the principal tenants of his great feudal magnates at Salisbury it seems that Little Domesday was complete. This was meant to be the draft covering Essex, Norfolk and Suffolk to later be added to the Great Domesday Book. Although the project was abandoned before these counties could be, that's rather lucky really because the draft has information the final copy would have omitted. The Little Domesday has 475 parchment pages and took 9–12 weeks to write up by about six scribes, which is an incredible speed and achievement when considering the times. A survey of the boroughs and manors of England, this was a way for the new king to not only control his subjects, but also know how much to tax them. Norwic (as it appeared) was recorded as having approximately 665 burgesses, 41 French burgesses, 2,100 sheep and 1 goshawk.[1] Herring also appears to have been of significance, and later in the thirteenth century Norwich had an obligation to provide the Crown with twenty-five herring pies annually. Nearby Great Yarmouth's coat of arms featured three herrings, a sure sign of their local importance to the economy.

24 September

This day saw the dedication of Norwich Cathedral to the Holy Trinity and 24 September has been annually celebrated ever since. The building of Norwich Cathedral began with the laying of the foundation stone in 1096 under the first Bishop of Norwich, Herbert de Losinga, essentially as penance for buying the diocese of Thetford in a blatant act of Simony. At the time it was the largest building in East Anglia.

Retaining most of the original ground plan with minimal alterations, today it is the most complete Norman place of worship to visit in the UK. This doesn't mean that over the years it hasn't had its disasters; lightning strike, fire, riot and war have all left their mark over time, but repairs and remodelling has left Norwich with a beautiful mix of Norman, Romanesque and Gothic architecture. Walking through the city, the spire atop the Norman tower (whose history reads a little like that of *The Three Little Pigs*, the first incarnation being made of wood, the second of stone and the final of brick) dominates the skyline and is the second highest in England after Salisbury Cathedral. An amazing array of carved stone bosses are found throughout, many of them retaining their colour, and totalling over 1,000. The precinct, originally built to provide support for the Benedictine Priory, also survives in excellent condition. It is now possible to see six scheduled Ancient Monuments and sixty-five Listed buildings in this one close!

25 December

On this day Henry I celebrated Christmas in Norwich Castle. Despite being originally built by the Norman kings as a royal residence, it was never used as such. At the time of the conquest, Norwich was the third largest city in England; when William the Conquerer invaded he was quick to order the construction of a new fortress. Raising a mound some 21m high and demolishing at least ninety-eight Saxon homes, the new motte and bailey covered 93,000m² and moved the main focus of Norwich from Tombland, the old Saxon market place.

Norwich Castle was put to the test in 1075, but rather than defending the castle William's forces were besieging it! An alliance between three Norman barons, the Saxon Earl of Northumbria and Danes saw rebellion break while William the Conquerer was abroad. The rebel Ralph de Guader, the Norman Earl of East Anglia, was forced to flee to his home in Brittany, leaving his wife Emma behind to defend Norwich Castle. She put up a remarkable fight and successfully held out for three months, before finally striking a deal that guaranteed her safe passage to join her husband.

The year Henry I came to stay, the new stone keep had just been finished. The limestone was brought in from Caen, France at great expense and was built to withstand attack, with walls 3m thick at the base and over 21m high. This new castle was put to the test by another rebellion in 1136. Possibly due to it being used by rebels more than royalty, from the fourteenth century the keep was used as a prison and remained so for over 500 years.

25 March

Henry de Sprowston, the forester for the Norwich bishop and monks, was patrolling Thorpe Wood when a peasant led him to the corpse of a local apprentice, William. The body had already been discovered once by a well-born nun, but reluctant to entangle herself in the matter she had apparently ensured prayers were said before retreating to her convent. Not much more was thought about the incident and with little ceremony the boy was laid to rest. It would be several years before Brother Thomas of Monmouth investigated the story further and took up the crusade against the local Jews, accusing them of making William a martyr through ritualised crucifixion. He published his account of the investigation and the medieval murder mystery soon gathered a significant following, although it never really gained widespread popularity.

The story of William of Norwich is the first of a series of medieval accusations against Jews of ritual murder during Passover. The Jewish community of Norwich was very new and most lived in the Jewish quarter in the Haymarket and White Lion Street, located near Norwich Castle. Speaking Norman-French like the recently established aristocracy, there were frequent accusations of collusion between the ruling class and Jews, leading to rising tensions between the indigenous Anglo-Saxon population and the 'foreigners'. In 1190 widespread attacks on the Jewish population spread throughout England and on 6 February all Jews in Norwich outside the protection of the castle were slaughtered. A hundred years later Jews were expelled from England and were not officially allowed to settle again for over 300 years.

18 June

Hugh Bigod (also Bigot) burned Norwich in revenge for the citizens' loyalty to the king, holding the richest citizens to ransom.

Hugh had been given land and position by Henry II, but when the king's eldest son, Prince Henry, rebelled, Hugh turned on the king. Joining forces with Flemish soldiers that landed in England, Hugh's men and the mercenaries marched on Norwich. He had expected the people of Norwich to join him, but instead he found himself forced into attacking the very town and castle he had once ruled. His initial success in securing Norwich was short-lived as the king turned his attention to English rebels and Hugh, forcing him to surrender. As punishment King Henry II ordered the demolition of various castles belonging to the rebels all around the country, including Hugh Bigod's in Thetford and Bungay. Shortly afterwards Hugh left Norwich to go on pilgrimage, despite being over 80, and, unsurprisingly, died en route to the Holy Land.

5 May

On this day King Richard I (Richard the Lionheart) gave Norwich a City Charter. It is the second surviving charter; the first dates to around 1158 and recorded that King Henry II 'granted and confirmed to my burgesses of Norwich all the customs and liberties and quittances ... as they most fully and honourably had them in the time of King Henry my grandfather.'[2]

However, the 1194 charter was the first to refer to Norwich as a city, upgrading it from a burgh. Not only did this confirm the previous rights that had been held, but it also granted an element of independence: the citizens of Norwich now had the right to elect their own reeves, allowing them to be ruled by someone of their own choosing; quittance of toll and lastage (money to be paid at port to be allowed to load a ship); the rent for the city was fixed and paid directly to the exchequer, rather than through the sheriff of Norfolk; and other privileges. It is this charter that is seen to mark the beginning of self-governance in Norwich.

15 October

Pope Alexander IV confirmed the second foundation charter for the Great Hospital, established by Walter de Suffield in 1249 as Bishop of Norwich.

Hospitals first began to appear in Norwich at the end of the eleventh century, with one of the first being the leper house of St Mary Magdalen and the hospital church of St Paul, originally called the Hospital of St Giles. The patron saint of lepers, cripples and nursing mothers, St Giles was also meant to have sympathy for repentant sinners and those who died without the opportunity for the last rites to be administered – always a worry in the medieval period.

The charter set out the exact terms of the hospital. The main benefactors of the hospital were poor scholars, paupers and elderly clergy. Seven poor scholars who showed aptitude for academia were given a meal for each school day, and the opportunity to train as choristers. For the poor, thirty beds or more were set aside in the hospital and thirteen paupers were to be fed bread, a meat or fish dish, and when appropriate cheese and eggs in front of the fire. On top of this alms were to be distributed, and on certain days of the year bread given to all the poor.

9 August

It was on this day that the hostility between the monks of the cathedral and Benedictine Priory and the local citizens reached crisis point and broke out into a full-scale riot.

Tensions had always been high between the priory and townsfolk, ever since the Normans first arrived, with disputes ranging from disagreements over boundaries to the split of rights and privileges. Then in June 1272 there was an argument over taxes at the Tombland market and a mob formed, forcing the priory men to retreat back towards the cathedral. Although there had been violent exchanges before, this time one of the priory servants shot a crossbow, killing a citizen. The men sought sanctuary in the cathedral. Over the weeks that followed frustrations rose at the lack of justice. So it was that the second week of August saw the citizens of Norwich launch an attack against the cathedral, burning down the gates, numerous buildings and St Ethelbert's church. The attackers also killed a number of men then looted whatever they could find, including sacred objects.

King Henry III travelled to Norwich to deal with the aftermath himself. The ringleaders and participants were put on trial and thirty were found guilty, which led to their executuion. The prior had his lands confiscated and was imprisoned.

As a result of this, Norwich is the only English city to have been excommunicated by the Pope, with the citizens having to pay a heavy fine and build the Ethelbert Gate as penance.

7 May

On this day Pope Gregory X opened the Second Council of Lyon where it was decided that, in order to prevent excessive diversity of religious orders, some mendicant orders (those that adopt a lifestyle of poverty, mainly to serve the poor) would be suppressed. Four Orders of friars managed to convince the council to allow them to remain: Franciscans (Grey Friars), Dominicans (Black Friars), Carmelites and Augustinians. In Norwich one of the Orders that fell victim to this new edict was the Friars of the Penitential, nicknamed the 'Sack Friars' due to the rough cloth of their habits. They had first arrived in London in 1257 and in Norwich a year later, settling beside Elm Hill. Although they were allowed to continue with their work, they were banned from taking on any new members. Slowly, the Order died out until by 1307 only one brother remained. It was then that the Dominicans petitioned to be allowed to take over the site, and permission was granted on the proviso that they care for the last friar.

24 March

On this day Walter Eghe, a convicted and hanged man, received a posthumous royal pardon. Just over a month previously he had been brought to the Tolhouse, which stood where the Guildhall is today, and charged with the theft of cloth from Richard de la Hoe. There he was questioned, found guilty and sentenced to hang. Which he did. However, when they removed his body from the gallows and took it to St George's church ready for burial, he revived! Not wishing to drag him out from the church, a watch was set up and for fifteen days Walter sat tight, waiting for his opportunity. Eventually his moment came and he ran to the cathedral priory, seeking sanctuary until finally a pardon arrived. Two things worked in Walter's favour. Firstly, surviving a hanging was often interpreted as divine judgement, although this wasn't always the case. Secondly, the king was displeased with the way the officials had carried out his trial. There had been no witnesses to the crime and, at the time, Norwich had limited power to try criminals. The king clearly felt that the city had failed to follow the correct procedures, so he personally took the liberties of the city into his own hands. However, lesson taught, the rights were soon returned to the city.

18 July

The order was issued by King Edward I that every Jew in England was to leave forever. The Jewish community of Norwich was thriving and included merchants, physicians, cheesemongers, butchers and financiers. As a group they were very successful and financially contributed a lot, both through taxes and monetary support. Although some may have converted to Christianity in order to stay, the majority were forced to leave. In the lead up to this a Jewish man named Meir, son of Rabbi Elijah of Norwich, wrote poems about the persecution suffered. Here are a few lines from 'Ode to Light' (translated from Hebrew):

> We languish, suffering in the land
> And hear the brute's insults,
> And steadfastly do we endure
> While waiting for the Light.
>
> A heavy yoke on us they lay
> Commanding and compelling,
> That we abandon and forsake
> Our only hope and Light.

These poems have been preserved on manuscripts in the Vatican, Rome, but how they came to be there is a mystery.

Following the exile, it wasn't until the mid-eighteenth century that a Jewish community settled in Norwich once more.

14 February

St Valentine's Day was celebrated in Norwich with a great jousting tournament. It was one of a series of tournaments held in 1341, possibly to try and curry favour with those the king had alienated in recent years. King Edward III, Queen Philippa and their son Edward, soon to become Prince of Wales (and later known as the Black Prince), were all present. A royal ban was issued prohibiting any similar events being held elsewhere, to ensure high attendance. Although it isn't known exactly where this event was held, there is mention in the eighteenth century of one part of the Gildencroft described as the 'Jousting Acre', which this would have been one of the only places suitable in the city. In 1350 the Black Prince returned for another tournament with his retinue, costing the city £37 4s 6d.

Jousting began as a way for the knights to practice their horsemanship and skill with a lance to prepare for battle. However, as warfare changed, this type of training became less relevant to the battlefield and the sport evolved. The joust developed to became more regulated, with rules based on the chivalric code, and safety measures were introduced to help prevent serious injury, one of the first being to change the lance tip (coronel) to a less lethal design.

10 June

On hearing that the plague was making its way towards Norwich, Bishop Bateman abandoned negotiations with the French over peace and set sail for Great Yarmouth. On his return he was informed that his brother, Sir Bartholomew Bateman of Gillingham, had already succumbed to the disease. The bishop hurried to his palace in Norwich but quickly escaped again. Although he refused to return to Norwich until the pestilence had passed (the smell of rotting bodies from the cemetery next to his residence as the number of dead continued to rise must have been intolerable) he travelled around his diocese before removing himself to his manor at Hoxne. The Black Death lasted until spring 1350, with the death toll in Norwich estimated to be between a third and half of the population.

Eleven years later the plague returned to England and was known as the 'Pestilence of Children' since a disproportionate number of children fell victim to it. This was because the majority of adults who had survived the first plague had built an immunity to it, whereas the children hadn't. In Norwich the population fell from about 25,000 in 1333 to around 7,500 in early 1377 following the two outbreaks.[3]

27 July

A view of arms was called on this day for the leet of Conesford, and carried out by John Bardolf of Wormegay and the king's Justices of the Peace. At this time, the administration of Norwich was subdivided into four areas, or leets, which roughly correspond to the original four communities that made up the city. In 1181 the Assize of Arms set out the exact terms of the equipment each freeman of England was obliged to have according to status and wealth. Should he be called upon, each man was to bear arms in the service of the realm. In the thirteenth century it was expected that two inspections a year would be carried out to ensure the city could carry out its obligation.

Each leet was meant to provide roughly 100 men, which were then subdivided into twenty with a vintenar in charge of each group. For the purposes of the roll these were recorded into three main categories: fully armed, half-armed, and archer. It is a sign of the wealth of Norwich in the fourteenth century that not only were so many well equipped, but that it quickly adopted the use of gunners, a new technology in England.

8 May

While laying on her deathbed, Julian of Norwich had a series of sixteen spiritual visions. On her recovery she wrote down her experiences, first in a short form, and then in a much longer form some twenty years later when she had further visions. *Revelations of Divine Love* is the earliest book in English still in existence known to be written by a woman. A woman of deep religious conviction, her longer text was the result of many years of spiritual contemplation and tackled the problems of reconciling the existence of sin and evil with the notion of divine love.

From the writings of Margery Kempe, another contemporary mystic, we know that visitors to Julian's cell sought her advice. Despite this very little is known about her; even her name derives from St Julian's church, where she resided in her cell as an anchoress, a reconstruction of which can be seen by those who visit the city today. In the Roman Catholic tradition her feast day is on 13 May, unlike the Anglican and Lutherans who celebrate her on 8 May. Nowadays she is held as an important historical, cultural, literary and religious figure celebrated each year in Norwich with a week-long festival.

14 June

The Peasants' Revolt against the poll tax reached Norfolk on this day and began spreading towards the Fens and Norwich, where the rebels occupied the city, pillaging, destroying property and even killing. Henry Despenser, the Bishop of Norwich, was charged with suppressing the rebellion. His soldiers confronted and defeated the rebels at North Walsham. There Geoffrey Litster (also Lidster/Lister), the 'King of the Commons', was captured and hung, drawn and quartered. Henry's swift success in dealing with the uprising and previous employment fighting for the Pope gained him a reputation as the 'Fighting Bishop'.

A couple of years later the warrior bishop was at it again, this time leading the Norwich Crusade to aid the city of Ghent against the French. At the death of Pope Gregory XI in 1378, many of the cardinals refused to recognise the new Pope and instead abandoned him in Rome to set up a rival 'anti-Pope' in Avignon, France. Europe was split as the various countries and states chose a side to support, with England choosing Rome and France Avignon, naturally. So it was that Despenser headed to France. The majority of men with him had taken the cross, promising to fight in return for a pardon of their sins, and indulgences had been sold to raise funds for the crusade. It was a disaster and Despenser returned to England to find himself blamed for the failure.

28 January

Norwich was granted a royal 'Charter of Incorporation' by King Henry IV that made Norwich a county in its own right, separate to Norfolk. It gave the city the right to collect taxes and elect a mayor each year, replacing the need for bailiffs. This marked a significant change in the way the city ran. Up until the election of the first mayor there were four bailiffs, each one representing one of the four leets. Considering Norwich began as four distinct areas that slowly merged, it is hardly surprising it took a while for a single representative to appear. The charter also allowed the mayor to appoint four men to act as Justices of the Peace. They held quarterly sessions to carry out their duties, leading to greater local power through Norwich's own courts of law.

This new power and the associated bureaucracy that came with it justified a need for a new Guildhall. It replaced the tollhouse, but at a great cost. A warrant in 1407 ordered tradesmen to give their labour for free, this on top of taxation and donations. This can still be seen today (although much of the exterior is Victorian) in the centre of the city, next to the marketplace.

25 October

On this fateful St Crispin's Day, Norfolk's own Sir Thomas Erpingham commanded Henry V's archers at the Battle of Agincourt against the French, leading to an overwhelming victory. A successful military career had seen him knighted around age 17, fight under the Black Prince and go on crusade with the Teutonic Knights. When Henry Bolingbroke (later to become Henry IV) was exiled, Erpingham followed his master and upon his return to England played a prominent role in raising support. His loyalty and assistance to the Lancastrian cause against Richard II was well rewarded with many influential posts, the Order of the Garter in 1400 and a significant income.

There is much evidence of his influence within Norwich. The citizens of Norwich paid him 20 marks in recognition of the importance he held in the king's eyes. A lasting monument can be seen in the guise of Erpingham Gate, opposite the west door to Norwich Cathedral. Flint-faced, decorated with the Erpingham coat of arms, there are twenty-four niches containing twelve apostles and twelve female saints. Above the arch kneels a statue of an armoured Thomas Erpingham, although judging by his chopped legs he wasn't originally made to fit there. His role at Agincourt is also immortalised in William Shakespeare's *Henry V*.

21 February

At the session on this day, an indictment was heard against five men. They were accused of holding a school promoting heretical beliefs that ran against the religious establishment, and two of the accused had apparently broken into a church and destroyed an image of St Andrew. It was decided that the prisoners should be handed over to the bishop.

The Norwich trials took place between 1428 and 1431 and were conducted by Bishop Alnwick. They provide a detailed insight into the history of Lollardy, especially in East Anglia. The Lollards, forerunners to Protestantism, held radical views such as making the Bible available for all to read, the sanctity of marriage as opposed to celibacy, preventing the corruption of the clergy, and disgust at the reverence shown to the cross as a mark of Christ's suffering. The vast majority of Lollards recorded were from humble backgrounds and many were illiterate. However, that didn't stop them from holding an opinion or engaging in theological debates with their persecutors, often quoting from Biblical texts.

In 1401 the law '*De heretico comburendo*' was passed, sentencing all heretics to be burned. Despite this, the majority of first-time offenders were flogged and given penance, provided they recanted. If they relapsed, however, the punishment was final. Sentencing became harsher over time, and during the reign of 'Bloody' Mary up to fifty people were burned. In Norwich this took place at Lollards Pit, once considered an evil place to be avoided and now the site of a pub by that very name.

19 September

Thomas Brouns (Browns) was appointed Bishop of Norwich. Several years later he was involved in the 'Gladman's Insurrection', a continuation of the old feud in Norwich between Church and city.

There were various small disagreements, but the breaking point came when St Benet's Abbey at Hulme complained that the 'New Mills' were interfering with their production. An investigation was carried out and the citizens were ordered to demolish the mills. The mills were not only seen as economic assets but, as producers of flour for bread, part of the lifeblood of the city – and this interference was interpreted as an attempt by the Church to once again extend its control. After delaying the final confirmation of the decision for as long as the city could, an assembly was called and in order to stop the process, the seal was physically taken from the Guildhall. A riot ensued and wood was piled against the gates to the Cathedral Close as a threat of arson. The protesters demanded that a previous agreement over tithes was overturned and managed to hold the city for a week.

Enter John Gladman, who wasn't particularly important and doesn't appear elsewhere in the records. However, at some point he appeared riding through the city wearing a crown as the 'King of Christmas' – and apparently thousands of citizens joined them. Unfortunately this procession was used by the prosecution as evidence of insurrection or treason, claiming that Gladman and his attendants were making a mockery of a royal procession. Treason was a serious allegation and one that the city was determined to contest, saying it was no more than a traditional mummery. Whatever the truth, the city was given a big fine and its liberties seized.

6 July

On this day Margaret Paston wrote to her husband, telling him of the new property she had rented in Norwich and the building of the stables there. At a rent of 5 marks (£3 6s 8d) it must have been a considerable property.

The story of the rise of the Paston family is incredible; from yeoman farmer to knight in three generations. At the beginning of the fifteenth century Clement Paston provided such an education as to allow his son William to study law. It was on this foundation their wealth amounted and they took advantage of every situation they could – plague, war and marriage. William did well in law and eventually became a Judge of Common Pleas. He made an advantageous marriage to Agnes Barry, which increased both his social standing and land ownership. His eldest son, John, followed in his father's footsteps; first becoming a lawyer and then gaining more manors through marriage. He spent much of his time in London and became friends with Norfolk noble, Sir John Fastolff. Unsurprisingly, when Sir John died his lawyer (John Paston) was the main beneficiary. The families who felt it was rightfully theirs weren't going to give up without a fight, and fight they did! The legal proceedings almost bankrupted the family and when John Paston died, his sons John and John (it starts to get confusing now, especially since they were both knighted) continued to battle over the property. John the Elder spent much time in London and his mother blamed their losing Caister Castle to his neglect. He didn't surrender though, and eventually, when the Duke of Norfolk died, his widow gave up her claim and the king granted Caistor Castle to the Pastons. They had made it!

29 November

Shortly before his death Robert Toppes drew up his will, which included a donation of 3s 4d to every Norwich church. His beginnings are lost to history, but by the time of his death Robert Toppes had risen through the ranks to become a wealthy and influential member of the rapidly rising middle class. During his life he was mayor four times, a Member of Parliament at least five times, an alderman, married into the gentry and had his own coat of arms – the sure sign of a man of importance. His own rise mimicked the changing status of the city, from that of a middling player to the primary provincial city of England, in terms of population and wealth, of the sixteenth century.

The first sign of his role as a merchant in Norwich was in 1422 with the buying of the freedom to trade as a mercer or fabric merchant. But his lasting monument is Dragon Hall, adjacent to the river and well placed for those travelling in and out of Norwich. Built in about 1427 Splytt's, as it was known, was built as a trading hall for his international business. The 27m showroom on the first floor had a beautifully carved dragon, which is what gives the building its modern name. Altered and divided over the years, it wasn't until the 1970s that this amazing building was rediscovered.

14 February

'Right reverent and worshipful and my right well-beloved valentine'[4]

These were the words chosen by Margery Brews, a young and well-born woman, to begin her heartfelt letter to her fiancé, John Paston the Younger, a member of the well-known Paston family who by this time had considerable power and influence in Norwich. Referring to the feast of St Valentine as a romantic day for lovers, this is the oldest known Valentine's letter in the English language. It gives a unique insight into medieval betrothals and shows that there was a place for a couple who fell in love. Unfortunately John's older brother and Margery's father didn't quite see it like that. As one of several daughters, Margery was unable to provide a large dowry, nor was she an heiress, so for the social-climbing Pastons she didn't offer a great prospect. In the series of letters over February 1477 is a record of the struggle between the two families to settle on the financial arrangements of the marriage. Margery herself appeals to John and the love between them, saying that she has tried as hard as she may, but her father will pay no more for the dowry. It seemed certain that the match would be cancelled, but the couple's mothers intervened and the marriage went ahead later that year.

6 August

Born in Norwich on this day, Matthew Parker was educated at Norwich Grammar School and ordained. His rise through the religious ranks began while he was at Corpus Christi College, Cambridge; there he caught the eye of Henry VIII, who appointed him Anne Boleyn's chaplain. He made a good impression on her and, as well as advancing his career during her lifetime, she also entrusted to him the care of Princess Elizabeth, days before her execution. He continued to advance his career and personal life, marrying once it was no longer forbidden for priests to do so. He tried unsuccessfully to reason with Kett's rebels, but it is partly thanks to his insistence that the history of the uprising was written that so much is known about it today.

Although his authority was stripped during the reign of the Catholic queen Mary I, his patience was well rewarded and, upon accession to the throne, Elizabeth I immediately promoted her old spiritual protector to Archbishop of Canterbury, the only Norwich-born cleric to be promoted to such a position. Parker was a much needed moderate voice at a time when extremism and hype threatened to tear the country apart. As one of the principal architects behind the Thirty-Nine Articles, he helped define Anglican doctrine and to shape the Church of England.

His reputation for investigating allegations and delving into other people's private affairs is rumoured to be the origins for the term 'Nosy Parker'.

25 March

Fire raged through Norwich for four days, and then again in June. Like many towns and cities at the beginning of the sixteenth century, Norwich's buildings were mostly made of thatch and timber. It is estimated over 700 houses burnt, destroying over a third of the city and affecting the local economy as rents dropped to a fraction of their original value. Following the disaster Norwich sent Thomas Aldrich, Robert Brown and Henry atte Mere to petition the Privy Council to speak to the king and ask for aid. Henry VII lived up to his reputation as a Scrooge and help was not forthcoming. The city was slow to recover and even as late as 1535 there were reports of empty plots and filth to be cleared. The fires did have the effect of bringing in the ruling that buildings were to be covered in tiles.

Remarkably the Britons Arms in Elm Hill is one of the only timber-framed medieval buildings to still exist, probably because it stood apart from the rest in the churchyard. It is also the only known beguinage to survive in England. This was a group of women who devoted themselves to a religious life working with the community. Unlike nuns, they didn't cut themselves off from society and tended to come from poorer backgrounds, making them reliant on paid work and begging to support themselves.

14 June

Bishop Nicke visited Carrow Priory (now Carrow Abbey), a Benedictine nunnery that had been founded in 1146. Prioress Isabel gave him a favourable report and denied any debt, however some of the reports from the other nuns make for an interesting read. Complaints included the divine offices being read and sung too quickly than was right, breaches of silence going unpunished, some festival days going unobserved, and the lack of a clock. The aged sub-prioress Anne Martin and also Katharine Jerves also felt that the beer was too weak! The bishop ordered that a clock was to be provided by Michaelmas and addressed each of the other concerns, apart from the question of weak beer.

When King Henry VIII's Commissioners investigated Norwich's religious houses, they discovered corruption in sixteen, but not at Carrow Priory. However it was still dissolved, leaving Isobel Wygun to be the last prioress. Her rebus remains on the house she built, consisting of the letter 'Y' and a gun to create a visual pun.

2 May

On this day the Reformation reached Norwich when Henry VIII granted the charter that would see Norwich Cathedral change from prior and monks, to Dean and Chapter. The Benedictine Priory attached to the cathedral had been running for more than 400 years, but now the last prior, William Castleton, became the first Dean. Those monks who remained were released from the rules of their Order, including the wearing of the habit. Their new roles as prebendaries and cannons gave them the responsibility of serving the cathedral and praying for the king.

The 'King's great matter', or desire for a son, saw him seek divorce from his first queen, Catherine of Aragon. When the Pope refused to annul the marriage, Henry VIII broke from Rome and created the Church of England. This removed papal authority from England and allowed him to marry Norfolk-born Anne Boleyn. The Dissolution of the Monasteries also gave him the much-needed money to finance his extravagant court and wars.

7 December

On this day Robert Kett, leader and namesake of Kett's Rebellion, was hanged at Norwich Castle. A reasonably well off yeoman farmer of Wymondham, Kett raised an army to throw off the oppressive leaders of the people of Norfolk and Norwich. Attacking from the raised area of Mousehold Heath and swimming across the river between Cow Tower and Bishops Gate, his men overpowered the defenders and took the city. Soon the Marquess of Northampton arrived with 1,500 men and Kett quickly realised he wouldn't be able to defend the many miles of walls, forcing him to withdraw back to Mousehold. Attacking the city once more, Kett was again victorious and forced the Royal Army into retreat – all the way to Cambridge! Not keen to leave a rebellious force in power for too long, the Earl of Warwick was charged to subdue the renegade force and arrived with 14,000 men to complete the job. Forced into open ground, Kett's men were slaughtered and Kett captured. Tried and convicted of treason in London, he was returned to Norwich to be hanged on the same day as his brother was hanged in Wymondham. A local folk hero, he is commemorated by a stone plaque 'in reparation and honour to a notable and courageous leader in the long struggle of the common people of England to escape from a servile life into the freedom of just conditions'.

16 August

On this day Queen Elizabeth I and her court arrived in Norwich on a royal progress. Her mother, the ill-fated Anne Boleyn, was born at Blickling Hall some fourteen miles north of the city. She stayed at the Bishop's Palace, whilst her entourage (other than those closest to her) found lodgings wherever they could. Much entertainment was put on for the esteemed guests during their time in Norwich and many gifts were given. The gifts to the royal servants alone cost £36 6s 8d! The queen was recorded as going hunting on horseback and watching wrestling and shooting on Mousehold. She stayed for just under a week. As the procession left, city boys dressed as fairies emerged from behind bushes, some of them performing a short verse, such as this:

> Yea out of hedge we crept indeed where close in caves we lay,
> And knowing by the brute of fame a Queene must passe this way,
> To make her laugh we clapt on coates of segges [rushes] and bulrush both,
> That she shuld know and world should say Lo there the Phayries goth.[5]

The queen unwittingly left a lasting impression in Norwich, as her court was blamed (probably unfairly) for the plague that decimated the city the following year. Over one third of the population of Norwich died from the epidemic.

25 January

> This daye was redd in the court a letter sent to Mr Maior and
> his brethren from Sr Faunceys Drake wherby he desyrth that
> the waytes of this Citie may bee sent to hym to go the new
> intendid voyage, whereunto the waytes beyng here called doe
> all assent.[6]

Waits (waytes) were originally nightwatchmen who would pipe
at specified hours or in case of alarm. In 1440 three Norwich
Waits took the watch from the Feast of All Saints to the Feast of
the Purification of the Blessed Mary. Over the years this musical
aspect developed and the Norwich Waits became the city's
personal musicians.

So it was that Sir Francis Drake, a national hero following
the defeat of the Spanish Armada the previous year, requested
the services of the Norwich Waits for his next voyage from the
Corporation of Norwich as his own band. The city was overjoyed
to assist, as is shown by the expense the city spent in furnishing
the minstrels with instruments and cloaks. Unfortunately the
voyage was a failure, with Drake losing over forty ships and
many men, including three of the Norwich Waits.

8 March

Will Kemp danced his way into Norwich having left London on 11 February. His *Nine Days Wonder*, a pamphlet he produced afterwards, described the feat in detail and the journey along the way. Taking nine days to Morris dance the route with sixteen days' rest, he was cheered on by crowds, with some of them even joining him for part of the way. Approaching Norwich, the mayor suggested he should rest and allow time for dignitaries to gather and prepare. So it was that when he made his entrance into Norwich the city waits, whifflers, knights and gentry were waiting for him. A reception was held by the mayor in the Guildhall in his honour. However his overseer, one George Sprat who was employed to ensure he really did complete it, insisted on him repeating the last section, claiming that due to the crowds he had been unable to witness it the first time round.

Will Kemp was well known as a performer of jigs and as a member of Shakespeare's players, and helped finance the building of the Globe Theatre. He played a part in the creation and performance of some of Shakespeare's most famous comedic characters, including the nurse's servant Peter in *Romeo and Juliet* and almost certainly Bottom from *A Midsummer Night's Dream*.

30 January

John Mortere was set in stocks after drunkenly shouting at Roger Gaywoode, his ward's alderman.

The use of stocks, pillories and other forms of humiliating punishment were commonplace in early modern England. Not only did each town and village have its own set, but within larger cities such as Norwich, each ward also. This was so the culprit would have to face the scorn of their own community. When stocks were used the offender would have their feet locked in place to immobilise them and they would be at the mercy of passers-by. Depending on their standing in the community, those who found themselves punished in such a way could have rotten food thrown at them, be insulted, spat on, mocked, beaten, or even tickled. However, there are likewise cases of friends and family coming to the defence of the miscreant, sometimes bringing them food and occasionally setting them free – although if they were found out punishment was usually in the form of time in the stocks. Confined for long periods, the physical discomfort suffered by the victim and exposure to the weather should not be underestimated.

One particularly strange form of punishment was the 'drunkard's cloak'. Those sentenced to this were made to wear a barrel with holes cut for the head and limbs to pass through. They would then be forced to walk through the town, presumably in order to discourage others from becoming drunk and disorderly.

3 May

On this day Norwich gained its first City Library, the first public library in England to be established by a municipality in a building owned by a corporation. Up until this point libraries and centres of learning were mostly to be found in religious institutions and were inaccessible to the majority of the populace. Despite the invention of the printing press in the fifteenth century and the Reformation, change was slow, but the beginning of the seventeenth century saw a sudden growth of public libraries around the country. Norwich Library was set up in three rooms adjoining St Andrew's Hall. To begin with members were only allowed access to the books, but in 1716 books could be borrowed too.

In 1784 the Norwich Public Library, one of the first public subscription libraries in England, was established. To begin with this was housed in a room in St Andrew's, so was possibly linked to the earlier library, but then moved to its own building. However, complaints about the lack of new books led to the founding of the Norfolk and Norwich Literary Institution in 1822. For many years the two ran in conjunction, but in 1886 they finally merged to become the Norfolk and Norwich Subscription Library.

In 1850 the Public Libraries Act came into effect and in response Norwich opened the Norwich Free Library in 1857 and a few years later essentially inherited the City Library.

1628

17 August

On this day Margaret Crookbill received a warning that after the trouble she caused by accusing Merable Church of being a witch, any more complaints against her would see her on the ducking stool. This shows that despite the general fear of witchcraft and the hysteria that sometimes gripped those involved in the seventeenth-century witch-hunts, accusations weren't always blindly believed.

There were many superstitions surrounding witches and ways to keep them from performing harm. Various mummified cats have been discovered in Norfolk, where they were originally placed in the wall or chimney of a house in the belief that they would deter witches and evil spirits from entering. Marks of protection, carved or written in candle smoke, were put upon the beams or in the plaster of houses, and shoes also hidden to ward off evil. If cursed with sickness, one way to deal with the illness was to create a witch bottle using items such as urine, toe- or fingernail clippings, hair and iron nails. If a person was suspected of being a witch then proof was sought, usually by searching the accused's body for a witch's mark or a way for a familiar to suckle blood. Those found guilty of witchcraft could find themselves hanged, or burnt in the case of petty treason (the murder of one's husband or master).

3 May

The first Florists' Feast was held in Norwich on this day, with guests entertained by Ralph Knevet's play *Rhodon and Iris*. The play was addressed to the Society of Florists and caused trouble with the Norwich Puritans, who viewed flowers as frivolous and disliked the pagan association of the feast with Flora, the goddess of flowers. However, their disapproval failed to stop the fondness for flowers among the artisans and nobility. The Englishman's growing taste for florists' flowers in the sixteenth and seventeenth century has been attributed to the influx of immigrants from Flanders, many of whom settled in Norwich, and quite a few Norfolk families moved to the Low Countries also. In particular was the love of the tulip, and this feast coincided with the rise in popularity that led to 'Tulip Mania' over in the United Provinces (now the Netherlands).

The intense colours of the petals and unique shape set the tulip apart. Add to this a virus that created 'flames' of colour and they became the most sought-after flower. As with all examples of inflation, demand outstripped supply as buyers stocked up on the varieties they thought to be most valuable. The price continued to increase, to the point where estates were being traded for bulbs! Following the inevitable crash many merchants previously considered very reliable reneged on their agreements and simply refused to 'pay up'. At a time when trading practise relied upon a person's word, this was a worrying situation and impacted trading across Europe.

However, the cultivation of flowers with the aim of producing a perfect form of beauty inspired a tradition that has continued to this day, its most famous incarnation being the Chelsea Flower Show.

26 December

After almost seventy years the Walloon congregation was told by the Bishop of Norwich that they were no longer welcome. Arriving as part of the great immigration from the Low Countries in the sixteenth century, the Walloons had been granted permission to use the chapel attached to the Bishop's Palace as their place of worship. At their own expense they had done up the chapel, clearing it out, replacing broken windows and repairing the roof. Once it was back in working order, it wasn't long before the bishop and his ministers began using it again and eventually moved the Walloons out completely.

The Walloons had arrived in 1565 when Letters Patent initially allowed thirty Flemish and French-speaking Walloon weaver families to settle in Norwich, who were swiftly followed by many more. Known as the 'Strangers', their arrival, although not always easy, certainly saved Norwich from a slump in trade, and by the 1580s Norwich's textile industry was restored.

25 December

On this day business in Norwich was ordered to go about as normal; Christmas was cancelled. A law in 1644 had banned decorations, carol singing and seasonal puddings on Christmas Day. Then in January the Directory of Public Worship, with a new liturgy and order of service, decreed that all holy days were nothing more than festival days and were to pass unmarked. So it was that on Christmas Eve 1645 the ministers and church-wardens of Norwich were told by the mayor that they must not hold services or administer sacrament the next day.

However, the celebrations were not to go without a fight and the successive parliaments had a tough time trying to stop the day being celebrated. On Christmas Day 1647 there were pro-Christmas riots in Norwich and Ipswich. On 1 December the Norwich apprentices had petitioned the mayor to allow celebrations. Although he refused to give his consent, neither did he stop those who wished to mark the day. For this act of defiance, on 23 April the military was sent to arrest the mayor, but the city gates were locked and a riot followed.

There were further troubles in 1648 when ninety-eight barrels of gunpowder in the Committee House armoury were accidentally detonated during local unrest, creating the largest explosion of the Civil War and nicknamed the 'Great Blow'. It caused several deaths and shattered windows, as well as covering the surrounding area in debris.

17 February

On this day the Norwich court banned 'throwinge at the cockes heretofore vsed by boys in this citty.'[7] This most likely refers to a particularly cruel game of throwing stones at a chicken, the first to hit it being the winner. But why ban it? Although today such a game would be considered cruel, animal welfare was far from the minds of those in charge. This was just one of a number of games and sports banned throughout England during the times of the Republic. The Puritans were zealous in their attempts to reform society and believed that time not working should be spent in religious study, rather than in what they saw as sin or temptation. This was especially true when it came to recreations such as 'throwinge at the cockes', where the likely prize for the winner was money.

Gambling amongst the lower classes was rife and it was considered the place of the authorities and those in higher positions to ensure the working class were not wasting their time and money. Not only was it considered a sin by many, but rather more worryingly it could pull them away from their work and lead to a greater demand on poor relief.

24 May

Two weeks after Charles II had been proclaimed king in Norwich, thanksgiving was held throughout the city for the restoration of the monarchy and an end to the Republic. The return of the Stuarts was greeted by the city with the ringing of bells, bonfires, feasting and much merriment. Those in power wasted no time in proving their loyalty and were quick to carry out the order of the Corporation Act of 1661. The Act ordered the immediate restoration of officers dismissed on account of their loyalty to the Crown, and ejecting those who had replaced them. In Norwich five aldermen lost their positions, although only one of the original five removed for loyalty still lived. A gift of £1,000 was also made to the king by Norwich and in September the soldiers were disbanded.

A lengthy struggle then commenced between the government and city as Charles demanded changes to be made to the city's charter, changing the rights the corporation held over nominating candidates. The aldermen stood their ground, arguing that they had removed any disloyal persons and so there was no need for the terms to be altered. Finally a relatively unchanged charter was accepted.

28 September

Charles II and Queen Catherine visited Norwich, but as they both arrived separately it caused somewhat of a headache to the meeting parties. As the mayor and welcoming party awaited the arrival of the king, it became obvious that he was going to be too late for them to be able to make it across the city to greet the queen. So a decision was made and Lord Howard's sons, along with the town clerk, made their way to welcome her into the city. The militia lined the streets as the king made his way to the Duke of Norfolk's Palace, which had been recently completed.

After a great banquet at St Andrew's Hall, the king knighted the physician and philosopher, Thomas Browne. Able to speak six languages, his most famous work *Religio Medici* (Religion of a Medical Man) was published in eight languages. Curious about the world around him, Browne's house and garden was described as 'a paradise and cabinet of rarities.'[8]

His resting place was accidentally damaged by workmen in 1840 and his skull was removed. It was kept by the Norfolk and Norwich Hospital Museum for more than seventy-five years. A cast was taken before it was reburied.

6 September

On this day Francis Burges published the very first *Norwich Post*, the first English provincial newspaper. Relaxation of the licensing laws in 1695 opened up the opportunity for publications of newspapers outside of London. Bristol and Exeter were quick to set up printing presses, but Norwich realised the need for print-quality paper to be available in place first. A mill was set up in Taverham and Francis Burges saw the opportunity Norwich, as a centre of trade and industry, clearly offered. So, following his apprenticeship, he moved from London and set up his printers on Redwell Street. Burges died five years later at the age of just 30, but the paper continued until around 1713, first under the guidance of his widow and then another London printer.

Around the same time as Burges' death, other rival newspapers began. Amongst these were the *Mercury* and the *Post-Man*, which merged to later become the *Norwich Mercury*, the longest continuously printed local newspaper in the UK.

24 February

A lease was taken from the City of Norwich for land on which to build the first purpose-built asylum in England. Founded by Mary Chapman, the widow of the rector of Thorpe, both her and her husband's relatives had suffered terrible treatment due to mental-health problems and so she was determined that her asylum would be for the care of the mentally ill. The Bethel Asylum was built upon land leased to Chapman and she paid a total cost of £314 2*s* 6*d* to build the hospital. When she died in 1724, she left all her estate to a trust, changing the status from a private institution and helping to fund continued provision. The will also included instructions for how it was to be run and the patients treated.

Over two centuries later the Bethel Hospital was still functioning and the introduction of the NHS in 1948 saw it join with Hellesdon Hospital. Although no longer functioning, it was the longest running hospital in the UK for the mentally ill and seen as a flagship for treating those with mental health issues.

13 January

The probate inventory for Elisha De Hague included chocolate cups, coffee dishes and 'cherry ware'. Although his occupation was stated as a worsted weaver, merchant would probably be closer to the truth. These luxury goods reveal the material culture developing during the Age of Enlightenment.

By the eighteenth century the affluent middle class were a force to be reckoned with and Norwich, much like other prominent towns and cities, had its own selection of coffee houses. The first recorded coffee house in Norwich opened in 1680. A product of the Enlightenment, the coffee house was seen as a social equaliser where men from differing social classes were able to meet to debate politics and philosophy, and hear the news of the day. Of course, on the whole women were barred from this intellectual world. Merchants and craftsmen quickly realised the advantage of inviting clients to discuss business arrangements in the comfort of the coffee houses. In London specific establishments became known for certain goods or services, such as Lloyd's Coffee House on Lombard Street, which was so intrinsically linked to the business of maritime insurance that Lloyd's took the name when they moved and it has remained since.

In the next century tea drinking replaced coffee as the preferred beverage and it was well on the way to becoming a national pastime.

25 October

An advert appeared in the *Norwich Mercury*, on this day for the sale of canaries at the Bear Inn. Originally sailors from the Spanish Netherlands captured finches in the Canary Islands and kept them as pets. It is thought the 'Strangers' of the sixteenth century, Dutch refugees, then brought canaries with them when they first arrived in Norwich. Breeding these birds became a local pastime and by the eighteenth century the Norwich Canary, or 'John Bull' variety, had developed. Originally they were bred for colour rather than song and by the late 1800s they were mainly deep oranges and reds. Today they can be found in a variety of colours including yellow, white and cinnamon.

The first recorded canary show in Norwich was held at the Greyhound Inn in November 1846, where a canary club displayed 300 specimens. Breeding canaries quickly became a secondary income for many of Norwich's working-class households. By the twentieth century, the canary was so culturally linked to Norwich that it became a symbol for Norwich City FC and features on their emblem.

24 June

On this day Union Lodge No. 52, the oldest Masonic lodge still working in Norfolk today, was constituted in Norwich. Originally taking its name from its meeting place at the King's Head, it was renamed after uniting with Union Lodge in 1817. Twenty-three years later in 1759, Norfolk gained its first Provincial Grand Master, Edward Bacon of Earlham. It went on to become one of the most influential provinces in the country and even boasts King Edward VII as a notable member of the Grand Lodge of Norfolk. For this reason, it was given the unique right to send a dutiful address on his death, separate to that of the Grand Lodge.

In 1879 No. 23 St Giles Street (now No. 47) was purchased to be used as a Masonic Hall, where it still stands today. In 1906 Hamon le Strange, as Provincial Grand Master, opened a new Temple, subsequently called 'The le Strange Temple', and in 1928 the foundation stone for a further temple, named after Bishop Bowers, was laid by His Royal Highness the Prince of Wales (later to become King Edward VIII).

14 March

On this day Jack Slack the 'Norfolk Butcher' or 'Knight of the Cleaver' challenged Jack Broughton, the undefeated champion of bare-knuckle boxing for the past twenty years and a man who had been taught by James Figg, Jack's own grandfather. Broughton's influence on the sport has earned him the title of the 'father of modern boxing'. Following the death of one of his opponents from injuries sustained during a fight against him, Broughton realised the need for basic rules and safety equipment. It was due to him that a count of thirty was given to a knocked down contender, by which time he had to be up or the match would be over. The fight was delayed for a month to allow Broughton to prepare. Broughton paid Slack 10 guineas for the winner to take all the house takings, which added up to around £600 (roughly £100,000 in today's money). Lasting just 14 minutes and 11 seconds, Jack Slack won, earning the title of Champion of England. His Royal Highness the Duke of Cumberland oversaw the fight and, it is rumoured, lost £1,000 on it.

Jack Slack was born in Thorpe, Norwich, and was the grandson of the first English bare-knuckle boxing champion, James Figg. Standing at around 5ft 8in and weighing almost 14 stone, he probably served a butchery apprenticeship under John Browne in Norwich (hence his nicknames). In 1743 he defeated three local men, becoming the Champion of Norfolk, and in the following year he was sworn in as a freeman of Norwich. However, wanting to build his career he made his way to London where the fight with Broughton secured his fame.

22 October

On this day the parish of St Andrew's suffered from a fire which quickly engulfed the local Bridewell (essentially a prison), destroying all apart from the impressive undercroft and flint wall. The desperate inmates were released, one of whom aroused considerable curiosity from the crowd that had gathered due to the commotion. The man scampering about the floor was making such strange noises, was so hairy and of such a remarkable appearance, that it was said that some mistook him for an orangutan. His assumed refusal to speak caused many to suspect him of being a spy, but, possibly through a description of him in the *London Post*, he was identified as 'Peter the Wild Boy'.

His story began in the mid-1720s when he was found as a feral child in a forest in Hanover. Brought back to England and kept by Caroline, Princess of Wales, he was a court curiosity. The finest tutors attempted to educate him, but his slow progress meant they quickly grew bored of him and he was 'retired' to a farm. It was from here that he escaped and wound up in Norwich. After he was returned a collar was fitted, reading 'Peter, the Wild Man of Hanover. Whoever will bring him to Mr Fenn at Berkhampsted, Hertfordshire, shall be paid for their trouble.'

14 September

Norwich 'lost' the preceding eleven days from 3-13 September as the Gregorian calendar was accepted across Britain. This was necessary to align the calendar with most of Europe. The Gregorian calendar was named after Pope Gregory XIII who introduced it in the sixteenth century. It was originally introduced to account for the inherent inaccuracy of the old Julian calendar, as a miscalculation of the solar year meant an inbuilt error of one day every 128 years. Superstition and a general dislike of anything 'Popish' caused unrest. Some of those less educated feared they would lose eleven days from their lives, and others felt it was wrong to move the holy days.

Under the old calendar the beginning of the year was Lady's Day, 25 March. When the eleven days were 'lost' the officials were worried about the chaos (and loss of tax revenue) it would cause, and so they kept the financial year as starting on Lady's Day and then added the 'lost' days on the end – taking it up to 5 April and keeping it 365 days long. In 1800 they ran into difficulty since under the Gregorian calendar it wasn't a leap year, but it would have been before. Therefore they decided to move the year start from the 5 April to 6 April and it's remained unchanged since.

31 January

This day saw the Norwich Company of Comedians move from their original location at the White Swan Playhouse to the New Theatre near Chapelfield and adjacent to the current Theatre Royal, with their opening play being *The Way of the World* by William Congreve. It cost £600, with the money being raised through subscriptions from local businessmen and lawyers.

Ten years later an Act of Parliament for licensing the Theatre of Norwich received the Royal Assent, allowing it to be called Theatre Royal for the first time. In line with this, the Norwich Company of Comedians began to call themselves His Majesty's Servants. Jumping on the new-found prestige this brought, Thomas Ivory valued the theatre at £6,000 and divided ownership into thirty shares, keeping two himself and offering the other twenty-eight for sale.

The theatre provided a platform for contemporary playwrights to showcase their latest works and alongside Congreve, Goldsmith and Sheridan provided much of the material. However, classics also featured, especially when political events renewed their popularity. During the Seven Years' War Shakespeare's *Henry V* was subtitled 'The Victory of the English over the French'.

1 January

On New Year's Day William Crotch, at the age of 3, visited Buckingham Palace to play before George III, the Prince of Wales and the Duke of Clarence. A child prodigy, William showed an interest in the family pipe organ before his second birthday, but his true talent revealed itself when a musician friend visited the family house in Norwich when William was only just 2. The following day his father found him working out the notes for the national anthem; by the next day he had completed more of the tune and the day after was adding the bass! Word soon spread and the family received many curious visitors, prompting them to showcase his remarkable ability.

For the next few years he was paraded from town to town and contemporaries began to voice their concerns over the detriment this would have to his welfare and education, considering he was almost completely unschooled. In his autobiography, William Crotch himself remarked that as a child he was spoilt and cringed at how he must have appeared to others. Luckily he was found a position in Cambridge and by age 13 had written his first composition. At the age of 21 he was elected professor of music at Oxford and retained this position until his death in 1847.

27 December

On this day an exhibition of wild beasts went on display at the Star Inn, including a beautiful lion from Algiers and an amazing Siberian black wolf. In this way the beginnings of the circus can be seen in the form of early travelling menageries, performers and appearances by unusual characters.

Norwich was famous for having one pub for each day of the year, and so competition was tight. As the different pubs around the city fought for business, they would often provide entertainment for their patrons. A couple of decades earlier the White Swan had showcased an ox weighing more than 100 stone and in 1797 the 8ft 4in Irish giant O'Brien (real name Patrick Cotter) could be seen at the King's Head. A few years later in 1806 a tamed crocodile from the Nile met patrons of the Church Stile, the advert reassuring visitors that they may touch him without fear.

Other entertainment included cockfighting and prize fights, both of which the Norwich pubs frequently provided.

13 November

Born in Norwich on this day, Sarah Glover was a music teacher who devised the Sol-fa Music reading system. Running a local Sunday school with her younger sister, she recognised a need for a way to help those musically illiterate to pick out unknown tunes. She taught her pupils to sing using a long scroll of notes, or the 'Norwich Sol-fa ladder' (do, re, me, fa, sol, la, ti, do). The system itself has its roots in a tradition almost 1,000 years old, but Sarah Glover developed it into a comprehensive system. Simplicity was the key to this and in making it so, she helped music become accessible to all levels of society. Once she had removed the necessity for singers to be able to sight-read complicated notation, she was also able to teach those much younger than previously thought possible. In 1835 Jarrold & Sons published her music scheme. A copy of this reached Revd Curwen, who then developed it further into what is now known as Tonic Sol-fa. This became extremely popular and was adopted around the country.

In the film *The Sound of Music*, Maria teaches her charges, the Von Trapp children, to sing using 'Do-Re-Mi' which is based on the Sol-fa system.

7 October

The committee meeting minutes of Norwich General Assurance on the 'Establishment of the Norwich Fire Insurance Office', the city's earliest fire office, place Thomas Bignold as its first secretary. He was probably chosen for his political independence, not being affiliated with either the Whigs or the Tories, and thus avoiding any accusation of partisanship.

Just shy of five years later, after years of disagreements between Bignold and the directors over the direction the company should take, he left and organised the financial backing needed to set up on his own. So it was that the Norwich Union Fire Insurance Society was launched. In contrast, support came less from the local bankers and merchants and instead chiefly from the shopkeepers. Able to work freely, the business quickly expanded and soon had agents across Britain. In 1808 a life insurance office was set up and by 1821 the company had twenty-five fire brigades across England, the one in Norwich lasting until 1929. Under his sons the business went full circle and Norwich General was acquired by Norwich Union Fire Insurance Society. The company continued to expand, adapting the policies as necessary.

In 1900 Surrey House was built as the new head office, a magnificent example of Edwardian architecture and tangible proof of Norwich Union's success. Inside are works of art and curiosities, such as the skeleton clock and marble air fountain, an early form of air conditioning.

In 2009 Norwich Union was rebranded as Aviva.

14 February

On this day Lord Nelson received the sword of the Spanish Admiral Don Xavier Francisco Winthuysen who surrendered to him his ship, the Spanish *San José* (often incorrectly referred to as the *San Josef* in English). A few days later Nelson wrote a letter to accompany the sword to Norwich, gifting it to the city. Later that year he lost his arm and the following year the sight in one eye at the Battle of the Nile. He later used this to his advantage when during the Battle of Copenhagen the signal was given to retreat; literally turning a blind eye, Nelson and his crew continued their attack and were victorious.

Horatio Nelson was born in 1758 in the Norfolk village of Burnham Thorpe. He first attended the Norwich School in the cloisters of the cathedral and then Paston Grammar School in North Walsham, north of the city, before joining the navy at the age of just 12. In 1800 he returned to Great Yarmouth to a hero's welcome, with locals unhorsing the carriage and insisting on pulling it themselves! Addressing a crowd in the Wrestler's Arms, he proudly declared, 'I am a Norfolk man and I glory in being so'. The landlady begged his permission to rename the pub the Nelson's Arms, but he retorted that would be absurd since he had but one! His state funeral on 9 January 1806 saw thirty-two admirals, over 100 captains and an escort of 10,000 troops accompany him to St Paul's Cathedral in London. His final resting place was in a sarcophagus originally intended for Cardinal Wolsey.

31 March

On this day Olaudah Equiano, a freed slave and a prominent member of the abolition movement, died. Three years earlier he had spoken in Norwich. His autobiography was a huge success and he travelled widely promoting his works and the movement through lectures, talks and public appearances. He financed his books by asking people to pay upfront and he received 250 subscribers to his eighth edition (which was printed in Norwich) in Norfolk alone.

Norfolk, and especially Norwich, was one of the major centres of support for the abolition of slavery. Sir Thomas Fowell Buxton, Elizabeth Fry's brother-in-law, was an abolitionist who worked alongside William Wilberforce. In May 1823 he introduced a motion in which he condemned slavery as 'repugnant to the principles of the British constitution and of the Christian religion' and called for its abolition in the British colonies. Ten years later he achieved his goal, and slavery was officially outlawed throughout the British Empire (excluding India where it was considered part of the culture), emancipating 700,000 slaves including those held in the West Indies. Buxton never gave up trying to abolish the slave trade across the world and continued to pressure the British Government to use its power and influence, even after he left Parliament. A plaque in Norwich Cathedral is dedicated to him.

7 May

Stoke Mills near Norwich. Jeremiah Colman having taken the stock and trade lately carried on by Mr Edward Ames, respectfully informs his customers and the public in general that he will continue the manufacturing of mustard, and he takes leave to assure those who may be pleased to favour him with their orders that they shall be supplied in such a manner as cannot fail to secure their approbation.[9]

This advert appeared in the *Norfolk Chronicle* and so started Colman's Mustard. After commencing his career in the flour business, in 1814 Jeremiah Colman opened Stoke Mill just south of Norwich and moved over to manufacturing mustard. Jeremiah and his adopted nephew James established J. & J. Colman, which was carried on by James' son, Jeremiah. In the 1850s a large factory on Carrow Road was bought and soon after the iconic red and yellow packaging and bull's head logo developed. The brand gained prestige, especially when in 1866 Queen Victoria awarded a Royal Warrant as 'Manufacturers to Her Majesty', which is still proudly displayed.

Over the years Colman's pioneered philanthropic ideas for employees including a subsidised school for children and a nurse for those who fell ill. Other benefits included an on-site kitchen that provided a hot lunch at cost, affordable accommodation and free educational classes for employees. A clothing club, savings scheme and insurance against sickness or injury helped workers to manage their finances. Upon Jeremiah James Colman's death in 1898, the £2,000 left in his will to the employee's trust was used to start a pension fund.

24 August

On this day Princess Charlotte declared that she would wear and promote the coloured bombazines (a type of fabric) produced in Norwich. Mr William Williment was appointed official manufacturer to Her Royal Highness. Ironically just over a year later, the news of her untimely death reached Norwich and was followed by a rush from the London houses, eager to buy up all the black bombazines that the Norwich manufacturers had on hand, as well as any other suitable material. The orders published in the *London Gazette* for the Court going into mourning instructed: 'The Ladies to wear black bombazines, plain muslin or long lawn, crape hoods, shamoy shoes and gloves, and crape fans. Undress - Dark Norwich crape.'[10]

In the following weeks the cloth manufacturers and dressmakers throughout the city were employed producing the orders that came pouring in for mourning clothes. From the moment of her birth Princess Charlotte had been immensely popular, despite the general unpopularity of the royal family, and this was reflected by the deep state of mourning the country fell into. On the day of her funeral black was worn generally and the Mayor of Norwich substituted his official cloak for one of black crape.

7 September

On this day Mary, the wife of Christopher Berry, and their six children were ordered to enter Norwich Workhouse.

During an episode of BBC's *Who Do You Think You Are?* it was discovered that the great-great-great-grandparents of celebrity chef Mary Berry fell on hard times. However, it seems that while his wife and children were inside, Christopher Berry continued his work as a printer while contributing to their upkeep. Even after the death of two of his children and with an apparently steady income, he continued to pay the workhouse rather than keep a household. What reason he had for this is unknown.

In 1712 the Norwich Incorporation of Guardians of the Poor was created for the purpose of carrying out the Poor Law. Comprising forty-two parishes and hamlets, it set up a workhouse in Bridge Street using part of the building remaining from the Blackfriars' Friary, and then another in the 1770s in the former palace belonging to the Duke of Norfolk. In 1783 around 700–800 people were supported in the Norwich workhouses at a cost of £10,000, plus £3,000 to support the poor living at home. Children in the workhouse were not only encouraged to learn to read and write, but also given work so that they could provide for some of their upkeep and have a greater chance of finding a job when they left. Those in St John's Workhouse were in the same year employed in spinning yarn.

14 June

Rosary Cemetery, the first non-denominational cemetery in England, was registered with the Bishop of Norwich, Henry Bathurst. Prior to cemeteries such as this, non-conformists were often forced to have their relatives buried in parish church-yards to the Anglican rites, with the fees financing the Church of England. Considering the history of non-conformism in Norwich, it is perhaps fitting that the city was the first to offer religious freedom after death.

The land was bought by a Presbyterian minister, the Revd Thomas Drummond, in 1819 and a board of twelve trustees set up. Some groups already had special dispensation for their own burial grounds – the Quakers, Jews and Unitarians for example – but this was the first cemetery to be open to all. By the beginning of the nineteenth century, Norwich churchyards were overflowing and Rosary Cemetery helped alleviate this problem, although uptake was slow. The first burial was the re-interment of Ann Drummond, the wife of the founder, in November 1821. Thirty-one years later her husband joined her.

1 May

Born on this day to a local artist, Antonio Frederic Augustus Sands exhibited his first picture at the Norwich Art Union at the age of just 10. Born on St Giles Hill and educated at Norwich Grammar School, his father's trade was originally as a dyer before he became a painter and most likely guided both Antonio and his sister Emma's artistic schooling. Still a boy, his professional life started in 1842 with a commission by J.H. Gurney, a Yarmouth banker, to paint an album of birds. In 1851 he exhibited at the Royal Academy and shortly after he changed his surname to Sandys, just before becoming acquainted with the Pre-Raphaelites through his piece *The Nightmare*, a parody of Millais' *Sir Isumbras at the Ford*. Throwing himself into the Bohemian scene in London, he attended parties, dinners and clubs, as well as spending much time at Dante Gabriel Rossetti's house surrounded by other creative minds such as Whistler and Swinburne. A carefully exacting and detailed draughtsman, Sandys was well suited to having his work engraved for print and his pieces appeared in several magazines. Also working in oil, chalk and crayon, in his last year he produced crayon portraits of five generations of the Colman family.

26 February

In the darkness of the early hours, prisoners James and William Brooks made a bid for freedom. Held in Norwich Castle whilst awaiting trial, they had used ripped-up blankets and rugs to fashion a rope. They managed to escape, making it to the top of Bigod's Tower, where William was the first to attempt to descend. Unfortunately the rope snapped, dropping him some 70ft. Remarkably he survived, although he did break his thigh, pelvis, arm and ribs on his left side. Both were charged with robbery, but William was unable to attend the first trial. The judge found James guilty, but postponed sentencing him. Later that year William was brought to the Norfolk Assizes for trial and, once again, although found guilty, his sentence was delayed. Both men were sentenced to death, and both managed to avoid it! James was transported and William spent the rest of his life in a prison hulk moored off Portsmouth.

16 June

The last Guild Day was celebrated in Norwich after the city was forced to cut its spending.

The day could trace its roots back to the fourteenth century when the Guild of St George was founded in Norwich as a religious organisation. It introduced an annual procession, the Guild Day, on the feast day of St George – 23rd April. Prominent characters included St George, Margaret (the fair maiden he rescues) and the dragon – Norwich's very own Snap, which quickly established himself as the star of the show. Developing ties with the local magnates of the day, the guild quickly rose in wealth and power. The Reformation saw the abolition of guilds and in Norwich the Guild of St George was the only one to remain. By the late sixteenth century the celebration had lost its religious meaning and merged with the swearing in of the new mayor. An ingenious contraption worn by a performer, Snap would breathe smoke and, with wings flapping, taunt onlookers. Snap remained even when St George himself was forced to retire. Even after the last Guild Day in 1835, for a short time Snap continued to make an appearance at civic celebrations, but eventually he also disappeared.

However, that isn't the end of Snap. In 2009 Norwich HEART held its first Dragon Festival in 2009 – with Snap at the centre of the celebrations.

1 March

On this day the first patrol of the new Norwich City Police Force took place. England was quite a bit behind the rest of Europe, and even the Scots and Irish developed a police force first. As usual it was London that led the way in England, with London's Metropolitan Police established in 1829, but it took another six years for the Municipal Reform Act to prompt Norwich to follow. Dressed in blue uniforms with leather top hats, the force numbered just eighteen at the beginning, plus thirty-two night-watchmen. The first police station was in the Guildhall, but as the force increased other premises were needed across the city. In 1871 the top hat was replaced by an early version of the now iconic helmet.

In 1968 it amalgamated with Great Yarmouth Borough Police and the Norfolk Constabulary to form Norfolk Joint Constabulary, but in 1974 it was decided that the name Norfolk Constabulary would serve better. The headquarters are now at Wymondham.

23 November

Born on this day in London, Joseph Leycester Lyne was to later become known as Father Ignatius. Considered rather eccentric and overly pious, he pushed for the introduction of monasticism in the Church of England. Despite being an Anglican, his preference for high church tradition saw him favour many Catholic practices and attempt to reintroduce them. He was fascinated with religious orders and founded the Society of the Love of Jesus. While in Belgium, he took the opportunity to visit monasteries and convents, studying their rules and adopting a monastic habit. Upon his return to England he refused to stop wearing his habit, which saw him resign. Now calling himself Father Ignatius, he attempted to establish a monastic community in Ipswich, but was forced to move and set up his monastery in Elm Hill, Norwich. He even tried to build an abbey in the city. He faced growing resistance and, due to a mistake in the title deeds, Elm Hill was dispersed. He spent some time wandering the country before building an abbey in South Wales. An unconventional and charismatic preacher, there were even stories of miracles and visions. He died in 1908 and it is said that his ghost can be seen wandering through Elm Hill, cursing those unfortunate enough to meet him.

1 May

The first train in Norfolk to carry passengers left Great Yarmouth at 8 a.m. on this day, heading into Norwich. Since the opening of the Stockton & Darlington Railway in 1825, every town and city wanted to join the new transport craze and have a railway. In 1842 the Yarmouth & Norwich Railway company was created. As the trade port of Norwich and an increasingly popular seaside resort, Yarmouth was a natural choice of partner for the first route in Norfolk. Work began in April 1843 and took a total of 1,500 men to complete, with the formal opening of Norwich station occurring approximately a year later on 30 April 1844.

On this day 200 privileged guests travelled by train from Norwich at 10.30 a.m., leaving to the sounds of a brass band playing 'See the Conquering Hero Comes'. Taking 50 minutes, third-class passengers were left unprotected against the elements and without seats. The new railway brought commercial benefits to Norwich too, with roughly 60cwt of tea and coffee brought by rail in August 1844 for Messrs Wolton & Co. alone. In December 1845 the Trowse swing bridge was completed, making a direct journey from Yarmouth to London possible and cutting the time, compared to travelling by stagecoach, in half. Modernisation had arrived and by 1882 Norwich had three stations: Thorpe, Victoria and City.

12 October

It was on this day that Elizabeth Fry (*née* Gurney) – Quaker, social reformer, philanthropist and an 'angel of prison' – died from a stroke.

Elizabeth was born in 1780 into a prominent Quaker and banking family; her father was a partner of Gurney's Bank (Norwich) and her mother a member of the Barclay family. Her childhood home was Earlham Hall (now part of the University of East Anglia) where she enjoyed a prosperous upbringing. She dedicated her life to philanthropic work, which began when she was young with frequent visits to the poor, collecting unwanted clothes and helping form a class to teach children to read.

After she married she moved to London where she visited Newgate Prison. Horrified by the state she found it in, especially for women and children, she made it her life's mission to draw the public's attention to their plight and see conditions improve. Becoming an advocate of prisoners' rights and the need for education, she travelled widely to assess prisons and bring issues to the attention of local authorities.

Her work wasn't limited to prisoners; she also helped the homeless, opened a training school for nurses (some of whom went on to assist Florence Nightingale), and later in life she was involved in the campaign to abolish slavery. Through her work she met many other influential people, including another great woman of her age – Queen Victoria.

Literally noteworthy, in 2001 Elizabeth Fry appeared on the Bank of England's £5 notes.

3 April

The first patients were admitted to the Jenny Lind Infirmary for Sick Children, making Norwich the second city in the country to have a dedicated children's hospital. The first was London with the Great Ormond Street Hospital for Children.

Jenny Lind was a Swedish opera singer and philanthropist. Known as the 'Swedish Nightingale', she was popular across Europe. In 1847 she gave her first concert in Norwich, returning in 1849 to give two more in St Andrew's Hall. The money raised was donated for the good of sick children and paid for the initial running costs of the hospital, including the purchase of a property in Pottergate Street and the work to convert it. For the next seventy-five years it was run as an independent voluntary hospital. Its management then came under the Norfolk and Norwich Hospital, although it remained at a separate site. Eventually it moved to the Norfolk and Norwich in the 1970s, becoming the children's ward.

The Jenny Lind provided much-needed support for the poor community, with many of the inpatients suffering from the side-effects of unhygienic and dangerous living conditions. As well as providing medical treatment, the provision of nutritious food, rest and good sanitary practices probably had just as much effect, if not a greater one, on the health of the patients. From the late nineteenth century surgical procedures were on the increase and were, by the early twentieth century, the primary reason for admission.

1 December

A new fountain installed on the corner of St George's Colegate churchyard was announced in *The Builder*. Engraved upon it were the words:

> Wayfaring man, for thee this faucet was given
> A channel to impart the boon of Heaven
> Drink, and thank God! and in this water trace
> As earnest of His love, and emblem of His grace.

This was one of many new public fountains to be built in Norwich at this time, in response to increasing awareness of the importance of easy access to clean water. A report by the General Board of Health in 1851 noted that the Wensum was polluted with domestic and industrial waste. Thankfully the abundance of alehouses in Norwich provided a suitable, and healthier, alternative for Norwich's poor.

In 1854 John Snow had discovered that cholera was spread through contaminated drinking water and a philanthropic movement began to provide clean and safe water. Charles Melly investigated the plight of fresh water for dock workers in his home town of Liverpool and discovered their only real option was the public house, and so began a campaign to set up taps near the docks. These proved so popular they soon appeared all over the city. His ideas spread and at the end of the 1850s Melly presented one of his drinking fountains to Norwich.

13 February

Of this particular Valentine's Eve Helen Downes wrote, 'We do not here content ourselves with lace-cut papers, but everybody sends everybody real presents anonymously; and, as on all gift-bestowing occasions, the children come in for the lion-share.'[11] For those who think commercialism is a modern phenomenon, think again. In Victorian Norwich the weeks before Valentine's Eve were filled with businesses advertising gifts such as vases, tea caddies, cabinet goods, jewellery, perfumes, etc.

But the real magic came in the guise of Jack Valentine, also known around the county as Old Father Valentine or sometimes Old Mother Valentine. On Valentine's Eve Jack Valentine was known to travel from doorstep to doorstep, leaving gifts in his wake. In this way lovers would exchange presents, and parents would leave gifts for children. The lucky recipient would hear a rat-a-tat-tat on the door, and when they opened it the mysterious 'Jack' would have disappeared into thin air, leaving behind a surprise.

On a rather more cruel note, Snatch Valentine was also known to make an appearance. If you were visited by this character, when you reached for the present it would leap away from you as the hidden perpetrator tugged a piece of string attached to it, snatching your present away.

4 May

On this day Pablo Fanque, Britain's first black circus performer and owner, died. Born as William Darby in St Stephen's parish of Norwich, very little is known about his early life, although it seems he was orphaned at a young age and apprenticed to William Batty and his travelling circus. His first known appearance in the circus ring was on 26 December 1821 and his skills included both equestrian and rope-walking feats. He remained with William Batty's company for twenty years before leaving to found his own circus. Travelling north with the famous clown W.F. Wallet and two horses, Fanque erected a circus in Wakefield. In 1847 he made his very successful London debut, and afterwards established his troupe in Manchester. He travelled all around the British Isles and his shows consistently performed to full houses.

When he died a band playing the 'Dead March' led the procession, which included Fanque's favourite horse, four coaches and mourners. However, his fame doesn't end there. In 1967 he was immortalised when the Beatles released 'Being for the Benefit of Mr Kite', a song heavily inspired by one of Fanque's circus posters.

8 October

When Herbert Edward Witard was born in Suffolk on this day to a poor family, little could they have dreamed he would become the first Labour Lord Mayor of Norwich.

Shortly after his birth his family moved to Norwich, but when his father died when Witard was 6, the family were forced to rely on poor relief. At the age of 10 Witard was to be found selling newspapers on the corner of London Street, poorly clothed and wearing worn-out boots. Finishing school at 12, he worked first in Great Yarmouth as a cabin boy, and then in the boot and shoe trade in Norwich. It was there he built up a reputation as the best turnshoe maker, but his experiences of working conditions convinced him action needed to be taken. He was involved in setting up the Independent Labour Party (ILP) in Norwich and spent some time in London, walking there rather than taking the train in order to save money.

His political career in Norwich began in 1903 when he became the first city councillor of the Norwich ILP. Apart from a four-year break, he remained on the council until his resignation in 1951. He also served as a magistrate and alderman, as well as being involved in groups focused on helping those in financial difficulty.

It was 1927 when he became Lord Mayor, the first year an allowance was given rather than the cost of entertainment coming from the mayor's own pocket. An incredible tale of rags to riches in this very city.

19 September

A brand new roller-skating rink was opened at 8 p.m. on St Giles' Street, to which 1,000 citizens were invited. Costing around £9,000 to build, the entrance to the rink was found at the end of a covered passageway with a path illuminated by gas light and lined with rocks and ferns leading to a waterfall. However, in less than nine months it was necessary to expand the repertoire as the local interest in skating alone wasn't enough to keep the business afloat. This still wasn't enough and it was forced to close, reopening as a Vaudeville Theatre. The variety acts failed to bring in enough audiences and by the early 1880s it was being used as the meeting place of the Norwich branch of the Salvation Army. By this time the building was in such disrepair that members were forced to open umbrellas inside when it rained. There was the possibility of the Salvation Army purchasing the old rink to be used as headquarters, but the price was too high. By the end of the nineteenth century the building had been relegated to use as a warehouse.

The building is now occupied by Country and Eastern, a fascinating shop well worth visiting for its eclectic mix of offerings. It is also home to the South Asian Decorative Arts and Crafts Collection, the exhibitions of which can be seen for free at the old skating rink.

24 November

On this day Jarrold & Sons bought the rights to Anna Sewell's book *Black Beauty*. An accident at the age of 14 saw Anna Sewell injure both her ankles. Unfortunately she never recovered and was unable to walk or stand for a long period of time for the rest of her life. She gained a sense of freedom through horses, often driving her father on a horse and trap to the station for his commute. Her own limitations and dependence on horses for mobility gave her a great respect for them and the drive to bring awareness of the cruel working conditions some of them were put under.

The novel was presented from the first-person perspective of Black Beauty and was written in such a style as to encourage the reader to relate to the horses in the novel and sympathise with their plight. Although it is now thought of as a children's classic, originally it was written for adults.

The novel was written over six years, during which time Anna Sewell's health was in rapid decline, with her often bed-bound and reliant on the care of her mother. Five months after her book was published she succumbed to her illness, just long enough to see her book become a success. There is no doubt it influenced anti-cruelty reforms and improved conditions for horses. In 2003 the BBC listed *Black Beauty* as No.58 in 'The Big Read', their survey to find the nation's best-loved novel of all time.

1 July

The Norfolk Regiment was formed on this day from the 9th (East Norfolk) Regiment of Foot as part of Childers Reforms. Britannia Barracks were built in Norwich as the regiment's headquarters for the recruitment, training and accommodation of soldiers.

Founded in 1685, when regiments were known by the name of their colonel, the Norfolks saw service in the Caribbean, followed by India, the Crimea and Afghanistan. It was during the Peninsular War that the 9th were nicknamed the 'Holy Boys' after Spanish soldiers mistook the figure of Britannia on the badge as the Virgin Mary. The nickname, colours and traditions were inherited by the new regiment. During the First World War the regiment was awarded seventy Battle Honours and one Victoria Cross, and lost 6,000 men during the conflict. It became the Royal Norfolk Regiment on 3 June 1935 to celebrate 250 years since the regiment began and the silver jubilee of King George V. During the Second World War five men of the Royal Norfolk Regiment received the Victoria Cross, more than any other regiment of the British Army. In 1959 the Norfolk and Suffolk regiments joined to become the 1st East Anglian Regiment.

The Chapel of the Royal Norfolk Regiment can be found in Norwich Cathedral, decorated with retired Regimental Colours and with memorials to the fallen.

13 April

The first proper meeting of the Norfolk County Council was held on this day at the Shirehall. Previously Norfolk was administrated by the justices of the peace, although many of the 'new' councillors already held office. The electoral record for this election shows a handful of women in each parish as occupying property in their own right and so having the right to vote, at least in local elections. In the next local election five years later, a few women were elected to office in parish councils. The Education Act of 1902 saw the role of the county council widen as they took over complete responsibility for 157 board schools and the provision of the majority of funding for 341 voluntary schools. In 1903 there were more than 1,400 teachers across Norfolk. Female teachers outnumbered men almost two to one, but their pay was only two-thirds to three-quarters of that given to a man doing a similar job. However, one concession Norfolk did make was not forcing women to resign upon marriage, and in the case of Tom and Kitty Higdon of Burston, both worked at the same school with Kitty as the head teacher.

Almost forty years later in 1927, the county council moved its headquarters to Thorpe Road, Norwich.

13 November

On this day Norwich's new School for Technical Education opened on St George's Bridge Street. Founded by the city's civic leaders, it offered a 'recreative technical evening class for manual instruction'. The classes moved to Bethel Street for a short time before going back to purpose-built premises. Most of the students had to work full time, so the evening classes (and later the opportunity to attend on day release) allowed the students access to training. The first 100 apprentices in this way learnt carpentry, carving and cabinet making, all after a full day's work. Slowly it grew, first incorporating the Norwich School of Art and then the Norfolk and Norwich School of Cookery. In 1930 it became the Norwich Technical College and eight years later 'and School of Art' was added. Although the Norwich School of Art gained its own governing body and separated from the college in the mid 1960s, City College (as it was now known) continued to flourish, growing from its humble beginnings to become Norfolk's largest college of further education.

14 July

An international bazaar and garden party was held in aid of the YMCA, supported by many local magnates and businesses, including the Lord Mayor who opened the event, and Henry Trevor who offered the Plantation Garden as a venue. The stalls represented many different countries with stallholders dressed in national costumes from around the world. Visitors were treated to a selection of exotic imports, tunes from the Carrow Band and even fireworks. Despite the poor weather, the *Eastern Daily Press* estimated some 4,000 visitors.

The Plantation Garden project began in 1856 when Henry Trevor took out a long lease on a chalk quarry just outside of the city walls. Over forty years Trevor transformed the industrial site into a smaller version of the grand gardens typical of country houses at the time. In less than 3 acres he managed to include all the elements one would expect to find on the estate of a gentleman: fountain, rockeries, bridge and follies. Both the bridge and the summer house were built in a rustic style, as was popular with Victorians at the time. He even had several greenhouses built with boilers attached in order to keep exotic plants. The above event is just one example of the many times he generously opened his garden for charitable causes.

24 May

Norwich celebrated the opening of the Royal Arcade, a decadent expression of consumerism. Designed by George Skipper, the Victorian shopping arcade is an exquisite example of the Art Nouveau style. The walls were decorated with tiles inspired by nature and femininity, key features of the style, whilst the high ceiling of glass and timber, along with stained-glass panels, created a light and airy space, all the while protecting shoppers from the elements. Restored in the 1980s, the Royal Arcade is regarded as one of the greatest architectural examples of a Victorian shopping arcade and still provides a shopping experience for those visiting Norwich.

George Skipper is the architect responsible for many of Norwich's grand buildings, including the Jarrolds department store and the Norwich Union headquarters, Surrey House. The poet John Betjeman described him as 'altogether remarkable and original. He is to Norwich rather what Gaudi was to Barcelona.'[12] Skipper attended the Norwich School of Art for one year and trained in London as an architect for three years before returning to his father's firm, where he announced the opening of his own practice by painting 'architect' above the door of his office.

17 June

It was on this day in the Criterion Cafe on White Lion Street that Robert Webster and Joseph Cowper-Nutchey, two school-teachers, met and formed Norwich City FC. Winning the Norfolk and Suffolk League in 1904/05, and being judged as a professional club by an FA Commission, they resigned and joined the Southern League for the following season. The original club nickname was the Citizens, with colours of blue and white. However, their new manager, in a nod to the local pastime of breeding canaries, began to refer to his players as 'his little canaries' and the press quickly caught on; 1907 saw the players turn out in yellow shirts for the first time and the colour and name has remained since. In 1908 the club moved grounds from Newmarket Road to Rosary Road, or 'The Nest', an old chalk pit that soon earned the reputation as one of the most dangerous grounds to play at: once the edge of the pitch gave way; players had to be careful not to run into a large concrete wall, and even fans weren't safe – in 1922 spectators tumbled on to the pitch when a barrier on the top of the cliff gave way.

The 'On the Ball, City' chant that is still sung today actually pre-dates the forming of the club and is believed to be the oldest British football chant still in use.

25 November

King Edward VII visited Norwich to lay the foundation stone for the extension of the Norfolk and Norwich Hospital. Rare footage from the time shows the occasion, including the royal procession through Upper King Street with cheering crowds.

The Norfolk and Norwich Hospital was first built through subscription in 1771. It had become clear that a medical hospital was desperately needed and the Bishop of Norwich wrote to Benjamin Gooch, a local surgeon, in 1758, but his transfer to London halted any plans. William Fellowes restarted the project with a meeting at the Guildhall and began subscription for a local hospital in 1770. Gooch advised on all aspects of running the hospital from the layout to the curtains, and two years later the first inpatients were admitted. Although there were no restrictions in terms of religion or politics on patients, in an attempt to keep a high 'cured' rate, those with untreatable illnesses were turned away, as were infectious patients and those with mental health issues. Except in emergency cases, patients also needed to secure a subscriber to pay for their care, restricting those who were able to access the service.

The original building was designed by architect Thomas Ivory and served Norwich until early 2003, when the last departments moved to other sites. The buildings are now converted into flats.

15 March

A report on the city wall was presented to the council at its meeting on this day, and included was a description of Cow Tower. This rather strangely named tower stands on a bend of the river Wensum, covering a blind spot in the city's defences its first purpose seems to have been to collect tolls. Early references to the tower call it the 'Dungeon' and subsequently the 'Tower in the Hospital Meadows', as it first belonged to the priory attached to the Cathedral and then to the Great Hospital. Extensively rebuilt at the end of the fourteenth century as an artillery tower, it is one of the earliest examples of this in England, and also of this type of brick building. Purpose-built artillery works for this period are only found in Canterbury, Southampton and Norwich, with Cow Tower being the only one to be free-standing.

It seems it came to be known as Cow Tower in one of two ways: sitting in the corner of a meadow called Cowholme; or, as it deteriorated, the cattle grazing by the river used it to shelter from inclement weather.

14 April

At 11.40 p.m. ship's time, the *Titanic* hit an iceberg, causing a break in the hull and the ship to rapidly take on water. The largest ship afloat at the time, the *Titanic* claimed to be 'unsinkable'. She had left Southampton on the 10th of April, heading for New York and taking with her many emigrants seeking a new life. Included on board were newlyweds Edward and Ethel Beane from Norwich, second-class passengers who had paid £26 for the journey. Edward, a bricklayer, had already spent time in New York and had returned to England to marry before heading back to settle in America with his bride. When the ship hit the iceberg the two made their way to the lifeboats whereupon 'the women and children first' policy meant that Ethel climbed aboard lifeboat 13, but Edward was left behind. Due to this and the confusion in trying to launch the lifeboats as quickly as possible, many left only partially full. So it was that Ethel reached into the freezing water to help pull out a survivor from the sea, to find she had saved her husband. Edward claimed he'd seen there was still room and so he leapt into the icy water to follow, making him one of only very few second-class male passengers to survive. Both of them reached New York safely, and remained there for the rest of their lives.

12 October

The First World War heroine, Edith Cavell, was executed by the German firing squad at dawn on this day.

Born in 1865 just south of Norwich, Edith was first a governess in England and then in Brussels. She returned to England to help look after her seriously ill father and decided to train as a nurse. Working for some time in London, including as a matron with responsibility for training, she eventually returned to Belgium as director of a new type of nurses' training school. Dr Antoine De Page and his associates were wanting to distance religion from the medical profession, believing their distrust of modern techniques was hindering progress. The reputation of the school, and Cavell, grew and soon recruits were applying from all over Europe. However, expansion plans were halted in late 1914 with the German occupation of Belgium. Cavell became part of a wide network of bourgeoisie focused on providing allied soldiers with hiding places and false papers to aid their escape. The clinic was used to disguise soldiers as patients, but soon the Germans became suspicious and on 5 August she was arrested. Accused of assisting the enemy and trying to damage the war effort, she was condemned to death, despite tireless efforts from the US minister in Brussels and international outcry. Following her death there was international outrage, especially as she had also helped German soldiers whenever she could. The Kaiser later ordered that no women be shot without his permission.

Following the war her body was exhumed and brought to Norwich Cathedral.

9 November

Ethel Colman became England's first female Lord Mayor with her younger sister, Helen, acting as Lady Mayoress. A member of the famous Colman family, her father and great-uncle had also served as mayors of Norwich. Ethel had also been one of the first female deacons at Prince's Street and was a director of the missionary society.

In the same year Norwich also returned its first female Member of Parliament, Dorothy Jewson. A suffragette, trade union organiser, advocate of birth control and author of socialist works, Jewson was the embodiment of the radical political movement of the twentieth century that sought suffrage for all and rights for the working classes. Her maiden speech in the House of Commons addressed the issue of extending voting rights to young women. Although she only served as MP for a year, she later served on Norwich City Council for seven years.

27 October

This was the first day of a week-long performance by the famous magician Lewis Davenport, at the Regent Theatre on Prince of Wales Road. He'd previously performed in Norwich in 1910 at the Hippodrome, where local press reported, 'A hit is also made by Les Davenport in conjuring. The magician of the party is a master hand at legerdemain [sleight of hand], and he is also accompanied by a droll fair assistant.'[13]

When Lewis first opened the doors to his magic shop in London in 1898, little did he suspect he was starting what would become a family profession for over 100 years. The Davenport name is now very respected and well known within the world of magic. The London shop is still trading and going well, but those in Norfolk can experience magic a little closer to home thanks to Roy Davenport, Lewis' great-grandson. In 2013 Paul Daniels visited North Walsham, a town just north of Norwich, to open Davenport's Magic Kingdom. The only museum of its kind, it houses magical wonders and curiosities including a rare first addition of *Discoverie of Witchcraft*, written in 1584 by Reginald Scott.

19 November

On this day 'The Singing Postman', Alan Smethurst, was born. In 1953 he began a career as a postman, but spent his free time writing and playing songs on his guitar, all in the Norfolk dialect. Six years later he sent an audition tape to the BBC at Norwich. Impressed, the BBC called him in and recorded his first songs. However it was Ralph Tuck, the presenter of BBC Radio Norfolk's Wednesday morning show, that financed the pressing of his first record. Ordering just 100 copies, in four months more than 10,000 had sold!

In 1966 he released 'Hev Yew Gotta Loight, Boy?', which won the Ivor Novello Award for best novelty song of the year and was featured on an Ovaltine commercial in the early 1990s. His local popularity was such that in Norfolk he briefly outsold the Beatles and the Rolling Stones and even appeared on *Top of the Pops*. His fame may have brought him financial reward, but it didn't bring happiness. He used whiskey to get over his stage fright and by the late 1960s his singing career was over. After failing a comeback a decade later and never finding love, he lived out the rest of his life in a Salvation Army hostel.

29 October

On this day City Hall was officially opened by King George VI and Queen Elizabeth (later to become the Queen Mother) in front of vast crowds. Afterwards the king made his way to Carrow Road to see a football league match, the first British monarch to do so.

City Hall is now considered to be one of the finest examples of Art Deco architecture and unusually has retained much of its original features and fixtures. No expense was spared in creating the iconic structure, with contributions from some of the greatest artistic minds of the time and the finest materials sourced from around the world, such as Italian marble, English stone and Moroccan leather – even the bricks had to be specially made. Two imposing heraldic bronze lions stand guard over the entrance. Bronze was also used for the main doors, all featuring bronze roundels illustrating the history of Norwich including its main industries, trades and the building of City Hall itself. The 365ft-long balcony and giant clock tower housing 'Great George', the largest clock bell in the UK, and the deepest tone in East Anglia, only added gravitas to an already imposing building. It is rumoured Hitler so admired the design that he ordered the building to be protected during air attacks, allegedly so he could stand on the same balcony as the monarchs when he conquered Britain.

27 April

On this night and two nights later on the 29th, the Luftwaffe bombers arrived in Norwich, destroying many buildings and lives. Called the Baedeker Blitz, it was named after the publishers of a German tourist guidebook to picturesque English towns and included Exeter, Bath, York and Canterbury. A month earlier a British 234-bomber raid had completely wiped out Lübeck's Old Town, the fire killing some 1,000 people. The Baedeker Blitz was part of Hitler's retaliation as he tried to break moral by targeting quintessential English cities. These cities were chosen as targets largely for their historical and cultural value, rather than for military significance. During these raids nearly 200 fires were started, 850 people wounded or killed and over 19,000 houses were hit in Norwich, as well as one of Norwich's oldest churches, St Julian's, being damaged. Local department store Bond's was destroyed, but in the true wartime spirit of 'Keep Calm and Carry On' the owner, Ernest Bond, hired a fleet of disused buses and within three days Bond's were in business again, selling what they could salvage from the car park. A makeshift restaurant was even set up in an old corrugated-iron building.

Throughout the war Norwich suffered many attacks with approximately 340 people killed, over 1,000 people injured, more than 2,000 houses destroyed and some 2,600 more seriously damaged.

19 July

The last execution in Norfolk took place on this day at HM Prison Norwich. It was a double hanging, with both Alfred Reynolds and Dennis Moore being sentenced to death for the murder of their pregnant fiancées. Although the cases were unconnected, both were taken to the Appeal Court on the same day and dismissed. Their executions were carried out by Albert Pierrepoint, whose father and grandfather also worked in the profession.

Robert Stewart, one of the last hangmen in England, was present and in his notebook wrote,

We thought he [Reynolds] would be awkward, but he behaved. He sang *Danny Boy* twice. He had played the governor at crib and won two legs to one. Prize was a bottle of beer. His minister visited him at 10pm and said prayers. Reynolds requested AP [the executioner, Albert Pierrepoint] not to use the cap. Moore entered and placed his own head in the noose. It had to be removed and adjusted properly.[14]

27 October

At 4.15 p.m. Anglia Television first went on air as an independent company broadcasting to the east of England. The first broadcast introduced viewers to the modern studios and facilities of Anglia House in Norwich, and gave the first glimpse of the Anglia Knight that was to become the logo for Anglia TV for almost thirty years. Spotted in a shop on Bond Street by Lord Townshend, the chairman for the company, the silver trophy had begun life in 1850 as a prize commissioned by William III of the Netherlands. A pennon was added to the lance along with the word 'Anglia', and it was shown accompanied by a short extract of Handel's *Water Music*. The Anglia Knight was retired in 1988, although it occasionally made an appearance during special anniversaries.

Without doubt, *Tales of the Unexpected* was one of the best success stories of Anglia TV. Launched in 1979, it was sold to more than seventy countries and managed to topple *Match of the Day* from its No. 1 spot in the ratings. Originally TV adaptions of Roald Dahl stories, every episode of the first series was introduced by the author himself. Over time other writers were introduced and Roald Dahl's involvement waned.

24 May

Norwich's County Hall was officially opened during a visit by Her Majesty Queen Elizabeth II. In thanks, a silver beaker was presented to the queen by the Vice Chairman of Norfolk County Council. The beaker had been made by Elizabeth Haselwood, the city's only female silversmith, and bore the town mark. Established in 1565 for use by silversmiths, Norwich was only the second provincial town in England to have its own mark. Silver production in Norwich was known for its quality, but it ended at the turn of the eighteenth century – so this alone makes the piece something rather special. However, Elizabeth did something almost unique upon her husband's death in 1684. Like many widows of craftsman she was allowed to continue her husband's business, but with one difference; she registered her own personal mark and all the silver pieces produced in her workshop bear her stamp of a crowned 'EH'. Her work was well respected as the following year she re-gilded the mace belonging to Norwich Corporation.

Elizabeth died in 1715, yet with twenty-nine of the 200 or so surviving secular pieces of Norwich silver holding her stamp, it seems she left quite a mark.

21 May

It was on this evening that the Ziggy Stardust tour hit Norfolk as part of the Superstar Carnival Week in which Monty Python's Flying Circus also headlined. The actor, fashion icon and music legend David Bowie took to the stage in a packed-out Norwich Theatre Royal. Such was the demand that the queue from the theatre reached all the way down to Marks & Spencer (then Woolworths). The following day the *Eastern Daily Press* reported that his performance had 'put the adjective fantastic to legitimate use'.[15] It's interesting to note that Bowie's popular hit 'Life on Mars' featured the line 'From Ibiza to the Norfolk Broads'. Following his death in 2016, tickets for a tribute held at the Norwich Arts Centre sold out within 10 minutes.

David Bowie had visited Norwich in the 1960s to play at the infamous Orford Cellar. Dark and cramped with just one stairway in and out, more than 300 people managed to squeeze in on the most popular nights. It was known as *the* venue to test a new line-up before taking it on tour. Other notable musicians who performed there include Jimi Hendrix, Rod Stewart, Eric Clapton and Elton John.

13 March

A new Catholic Diocese of East Anglia was created by decree *Quod Ecumenicum* by Pope Paul VI. The parish church of John the Baptist in Norwich was consecrated as the cathedral for the new diocese, giving the city its second cathedral and providing a seat for the newly reinstated Bishop of East Anglia.

The church was originally funded by Henry Fitzalan-Howard, the 15th Duke of Norfolk, and gifted to the Catholic community of Norwich as a thanksgiving for his first marriage to Lady Flora Abney-Hastings. The dukes of Norfolk have historically been Catholics, which in the past caused conflict with various monarchs, and he hoped this would assist in integrating Catholicism into the community. The site of the old city gaol was bought for the purpose and work began in 1882. However, the first two years was spent stabilising the old chalk mines below and then further problems arose when, ten years in, the duke realised he didn't have planning permission for the entire length of the church. Designed by architect George Gilbert Scott junior, the building is held as one of the finest examples of architecture in the Gothic Revival style and its grandeur even rivals the medieval cathedral.

24 March

This day saw the Canaries' first triumph at Wembley Stadium when Norwich City defeated Sunderland 1-0, winning the Football League Cup (also known as the Milk Cup at the time, referring to the title sponsor). The game was played with much excitement, especially after the 2-0 victory against Ipswich in the semi-finals. Despite Norwich generally playing very well, the only goal of the match was an own goal by Gordon Chisholm as the ball deflected off his chest. The team was headed by manager Ken Brown, and Steve Bruce was awarded Man of the Match. Celebrations of the victory took place with an open-top bus parade, but they were short-lived as both teams were relegated at the end of the First Division Season. Under normal circumstances the winning team would qualify to play in the UEFA Cup, but a blanket ban on all English clubs playing in Europe later that year due to the Heysel Stadium disaster stopped Norwich from competing.

Out of this match was born the Friendship Trophy, a testament to the camaraderie between Norwich City and Sunderland.

3 March

On this day a No. 26 double-decker bus fell into a 26ft-deep hole in Earlham Road, making international headlines. Jim Pightling, the bus driver, was just pulling away from Paragon Place when suddenly large sections of the road under the rear wheels collapsed. As the bus began to sink further, the passengers scrambled off before the road gave way completely and the rear end of the bus fell into it entirely. That wasn't the end of it though, as police then had to evacuate nearby homes, schools and businesses due to a ruptured gas main that was leaking vast amounts of gas, causing serious concern that an explosion may follow. The subsidence was blamed on a medieval chalk mine found beneath the city.

Following the news story, Cadbury's launched an advertising campaign using a photo of the stuck bus along with the tagline 'Nothing fills a hole like a Double Decker', referring to one of the company's chocolate bars.

25 June

The official bid for Norwich to become England's first UNESCO City of Literature was publicly launched on this day at the Sainsbury Centre for Visual Arts. Successfully gaining the title in 2012, Norwich became one of only seven worldwide, joining Edinburgh, Melbourne, Iowa City, Dublin, Reykjavik and Krakóv.

This status was given in recognition of the incredible literary heritage of Norwich (almost a millennia!) and the thriving community still present. The 'firsts' the city can claim include a battlefield dispatch in 1075, the first Jewish author in England, the first woman published in English, the first recognisable novel, the first blank verse, the first printed plan of an English city and the first provincial newspaper. More recently, the University of East Anglia was the first to offer a British MA in Creative Writing, with Ian McEwan as the first student, and Norwich became the UK's first City of Refuge, offering a safe haven for persecuted writers. The Norfolk and Norwich Millennium Library in the centre of the city has consistently proved to be one of the most popular libraries in the country.

19 January

On this day Norwich-born Martin Faulks made national headlines as the 'Ninja of Norwich'. A lifetime student of martial arts, Martin has travelled around the world in search of ancient spiritual traditions. For TV cameras, he tested his stealth against that of a jaguar; his meditation skills have been scrutinised by a computer; and the power of his mind proven through the demonstration of 'tummo', the Tibetan method of heating the body using meditation known as inner fire. Martin's interests, however, are not limited to the ancient masked warriors, and at the time of writing he is still on a quest to find the limit of human potential.

He has visited Japan several times to train with the mysterious Yamabushi monks found in the sacred mountains. Following the path of Shugendo, an amalgamation of the native pagan religion of Shinto and Buddhism, the rituals of the monks centre on mountains particular to each sect. Having to perform various tests, Martin has been hung off the edge of a cliff, endured standing under a freezing cold mountain waterfall at midnight and meditated in a chilli-smoke-filled room.

8 October

On this day the Enterprise Centre, part of the campus of the University of East Anglia (UEA), was officially opened. Famed as Britain's greenest building, UEA has a history of leading the way with award-winning, low-energy buildings, this being the latest to set new standards.

The designers took advantage of the latest advances in ecologically friendly technologies to create a dynamic and flexible space that has been held up as an example for what is possible. The carbon footprint was calculated to be 440kg/CO_2/sq.m across the 100-year lifespan, which is a quarter of that expected from a building of similar dimensions built in a more usual manner. To help achieve this it was made almost entirely from locally sourced and recycled materials, including beams from old lab desks, corsican pine stud work from Thetford Forest, 58 tonnes of recycled newspapers for insulation, and 98 per cent of the steel for the frame was also recycled. Some of the technology used is quite typical, like the solar panels that cover the roof, and some rather less so, for example the smart technology that constantly monitors temperature, humidity and air composition to advise when to open doors and windows. The clever placing of windows and reflective panels moves natural light around the building, which not only reduces the energy consumption, but also creates a more pleasant workspace.

18 January

After five years on the board of directors for Norwich City FC, it was announced that popular comedian, actor, presenter and activist Stephen Fry would be stepping down and instead take on the role of 'Norwich City Ambassador'. A long-time Canary fan, Fry notes that his love of the club was present before his love of sport in general.

Although Stephen Fry wasn't born in Norfolk, he is perhaps its most well-known and best-loved resident. His parents moved to Norfolk when he was young and he was a student for some time at Paston School, North Walsham. He also attended Norfolk College of Arts and City College in Norwich, from where he successfully obtained a scholarship to Queens' College, Cambridge. Fry is patron of the Norwich Playhouse theatre, and a puppet personalised by him was auctioned off by Norwich Puppet Theatre for its 30th birthday. Often vocal about his love for the city and Norfolk as a whole, Stephen Fry is one of Norwich's greatest advocates.

Endnotes

1   'The Domesday Book Online' Available from www.domesdaybook.co.uk/
    norfolk4.html#norwich [Accessed 6 November 2015]
2   Ballard, Adolphus, *British Borough Charters 1042-1216*. Cambridge
    University Press: 2010, p.8
3   Britnell, Richard (1994). 'The Black Death in English towns'. Urban
    History, vol. 21, issue 2, October 1994, pp.195-210, p.200 http://dx.doi.
    org/10.1017/S0963926800011020
4   February 1477 *BL Additional MS 43488, f. 23r*, www.bl.uk/manuscripts/
    FullDisplay.aspx?ref=Add_MS_43490 (modern translation by The
    British Library)
5   Dovey, Zillah, *Elizabethan Progress: The Queen's Journey into East Anglia 1578*.
    Fairleigh Dickinson University Press: 1996, p.85
6   Stephen, George, 'The Waits of the City of Norwich Through Four
    Centuries to 1790', Norfolk and Norwich Archaeology Society, 25 (1933),
    p.1
7   Quoted by Tonge, Dave, 'Throwing at Cocks. What's that all about?'
    The Shaming of Agnes Leman, April 2012. [Online] Available from http://
    theshamingofagnesleman.blogspot.co.uk/2012/04/throwing-at-cocks-
    whats-that-all-about.html [Accessed 2 August 2015]
8   17 October 1671 Diary of John Evelyn quoted in Hooper, James *Jarrold's
    Official Guide to Norwich.* Jarrold: London 1900, p.181
9   Mackie, Charles *Norfolk Annals: A Chronological Record of Remarkable Events in
    the Nineteenth Century, Vol. 1.* [Online] Available from www.gutenberg.org/
    ebooks/36206
10 *The London Gazette*, 8 November 1817
11 Downes, Helen *Norfolk Chronicle,* 15 February 1862
12 http://royalarcadenorwich.co.uk/arcade-history
13 From the Davenport Archive
14 Quoted in Pavasovic, Mike, 'Bus driver, licensee – and hangmen' in
    Oldham Evening Chronicle, 4 September 2008
15 *Eastern Daily Press*, 22 May 1973

Bibliography

BOOKS AND JOURNALS

Ayers, Brian, *Norwich: Archaeology of a Fine City*. Stroud: Amberley Publishing, 2009

Ballard, Adolphus, *British Borough Charters 1042-1216*. Cambridge: Cambridge University Press, 2010

Beatniffe, Richard (ed.), *The Norfolk Tour, Or, Traveller's Pocket-companion ... 6th Ed.* Norwich: Unknown, 1808

Campbell, C., *The Anniversary History: 250 years of Norfolk Freemasonry 1759-2009*. Great Yarmouth: Ashleigh Print & Design Ltd, 2009

Chambers, John, *A General History of the County of Norfolk*. Norfolk: J. Stacy, 1829

Dovey, Zillah, *An Elizabethan Progress: The Queen's Journey into East Anglia*. Madison: Fairleigh Dickinson University Press, 1996

Durston, Chris, 'The Puritan War on Christmas'. *History Today*, 35, (12), 1985

Harper-Bill, Christopher (ed.), *Medieval East Anglia*. Woodbridge: The Boydell Press, 2005

Hooper, James, *Jarrold's Official Guide to Norwich*. London: Jarrold, 1900

Hudson, William, 'Norwich Militia in the Fourteenth Century'. *Norfolk Archaeology*, 14, 1901

Hudson, William and John Tingey (eds), *The Records of the City of Norwich, vol. 1*. Norwich: Jarrold, 1906

Meers, Frank, *The Story of Norwich*. Andover: Phillimore & Co. Ltd, 2011

Rawcliffe, Carole and Richard Wilson (eds), *Medieval Norwich*. London: Hambledon and London, 2004

Rawcliffe, Carole and Wilson, Richard (eds), *Norwich Since 1550*. London: Hambledon and London, 2004

Rose, Emily, *The Murder of William of Norwich: The Origins of the Blood Libel in Medieval Norwich*. USA: Oxford University Press, 2015

Staff, Morson, *Norwich Murders*. Barnsley: Pen & Sword, 2006

Stephen, George, 'The Waits of the City of Norwich Through Four Centuries to 1790', *Norfolk and Norwich Archaeology Society*, 25 (1933), pp.1-70

Storey, Neil, *Norfolk Villains: Rogues, Rascals & Reprobates*. The History Press: Stroud, 2012

Summers, David, 'George John Skipper: Norfolk Architect'. In: Ferry, Kathryn (ed.) *Powerhouses of Provincial Architecture, 1837-1914*. London: Victorian Society, 2009, pp.74-82

Summerson, Henry, 'Attitudes to Capital Punishment in England, 1200-1350'
    In: Prestwich, Michael, Richard Britnell and Robin Frame (eds). *Thirteenth Century England VIII: Proceedings of the Durham Conference 1999*. Woodbridge: Boydell Press, 2001, pp.123-134
Tonge, Dave, *Tudor Tales*. Stroud: The History Press, 2015
Williamson, Fiona, *Social Relations and Urban Space: Norwich, 1600-1700*. Woodbridge: Boydell & Brewer Ltd, 2014

NEWSPAPERS

Eastern Daily Press
Norfolk Chronicle
Oldham Evening Chronicle
The Art-Union
The Era
The Guardian
The London Gazette
The Sun

WEBSITES

Boxing Monthly
British Library
Early English Books Online
East Anglian Film Archive
Encyclopedia Titanica
History of Parliament Online
Literary Norfolk
National Museum of Women in the Arts
Norfolk Record Office
Norwich Heritage Economic & Regeneration Trust (Norwich HEART)
Oxford Dictionary of National Biography
The British Newspaper Archive
The Domesday Book Online
The Royal Arcade Norwich

MUSEUMS

Davenport's Magic Kingdom
Museum of Norwich at the Bridewell
Norwich Castle
Norwich Union Museum
The Library and Museum of Freemasonry

About the Author

KINDRA JONES was awarded a first for her degree in History and now runs her own company – The Lady Knight www.theladyknight.co.uk – which specialises in historical re-enactments and bringing the past to life to audiences of all ages.

A keen local historian, she has worked freelance for Norfolk Museums since 2011 and lives in North Walsham, Norfolk.

Visit our website and discover thousands of
other History Press books.

www.thehistorypress.co.uk